COOKIE

CANVAS

COOKIE

CREATIVE DESIGNS
FOR EVERY OCCASION
AMBER SPIEGEL
@SweetAmbs

CANVAS

For the curious

Publisher Mike Sanders
Editor Christopher Stolle
Assistant Director of Art/Design Rebecca Batchelor
Photographers Amber Spiegel & Tom Moore
Recipe Tester Dana Angelo White
Proofreaders Georgette Beatty & Gail Stein
Indexer Jessica McCurdy Crooks

First American Edition, 2022
Published in the United States by DK Publishing
6081 E. 82nd Street, Suite 400, Indianapolis, IN 46250

© 2022 by Amber Spiegel
22 23 24 25 26 10 9 8 7 6 5 4 3
001-331514-OCT2022

Library of Congress Catalog Number: 2022934440
ISBN: 978-0-7440-6083-6

Note: This publication contains the opinions and ideas of its author.
It is intended to provide helpful and informative material on the subject
matter covered. It is sold with the understanding that the author and publisher
are not engaged in rendering professional services in the book. If the reader
requires personal assistance or advice, a competent professional should be consulted.
The author and publisher specifically disclaim any responsibility for any liability, loss,
or risk, personal or otherwise, which is incurred as a consequence, directly or indirectly,
of the use and application of any of the contents of this book.

Trademarks: All terms mentioned in this book that are known to be
or are suspected of being trademarks or service marks have been
appropriately capitalized. DK and Penguin Random House LLC cannot
attest to the accuracy of this information. Use of a term in this book should
not be regarded as affecting the validity of any trademark or service mark.

DK books are available at special discounts when purchased in bulk for sales promotions,
premiums, fund-raising, or educational use. For details, contact: SpecialSales@dk.com.

Printed and bound in China

Photographs on pages 5 and 7 by Tom Moore Photography
Cover photo and all other photographs by Amber Spiegel

For the curious
www.dk.com

AMBER SPIEGEL (@sweetambs) is a professional cookie decorator and one of the leading cookie decorating instructors on Instagram and Facebook. Her journey to this point in her professional career started when she enrolled in the Baking and Pastry Program at the Culinary Institute of America in Hyde Park, New York, to pursue her dream of becoming a professional baker.

During those years, she realized her true passion was decorating cookies and cakes— a profession where she could combine her artistic skills with her love of baking. Amber now creates cookie decorating video tutorials from her home studio in Kingston, New York, where she lives with her husband, Marc, and their daughters, Olive and Sidney.

Amber's work has been featured in *Martha Stewart Weddings*, *InStyle*, *Brides*, *Huffington Post*, and *Better Homes and Gardens*. She's been named one of *Forbes*'s Top Influencers in food and she contributed cookie artwork for Puffin Plated's *Pride and Prejudice*. She's also the author of *Cookie Art: Sweet Designs for Special Occasions*.

CONTENTS

CELEBRATION COOKIES.........57

ANYTIME COOKIES.........147

TEMPLATES...........195

INDEX.................206

ACKNOWLEDGMENTS...208

SEASONAL COOKIES.........93

INTRODUCTION

I've always loved baking, but I didn't consider pursuing a career as a baker until I was in my junior year of college. I was studying business administration, which I wasn't interested in at all, and my grades reflected my feelings toward my major. It was during that time I started baking for my roommates for fun and watching cooking shows, which is when I thought maybe I could do what I love for a living and become a professional baker.

After graduation, I worked as an office assistant for my dad at his woodworking business while I figured out what to do next. Living so close to the Culinary Institute of America and my dad being a former student of the school made it an easy decision to apply. Soon after, I was accepted into the Baking and Pastry Program and then started working at a local bakery to get experience in the industry before my start date at the (other) CIA.

It was such a huge change going from studying business administration to doing something I actually loved. I went from being a C student as a business major to getting straight As in culinary school. It turns out math is a lot easier for me to understand when it's related to food!

At the time I attended the CIA, the program was just under 2 years long, with each class lasting only 3 weeks, which meant we had the opportunity to learn a wide variety of baking and pastry techniques. This allowed me to narrow my focus pretty quickly to cake decorating. (Cookie decorating wasn't a big part of the program, but I took what I learned about decorating cakes and applied it to cookies later.)

Shortly after graduating from culinary school, I decided to try my hand at cookie decorating. I'd been making cakes for family and friends, but I wanted to make beautiful treats I could ship to loved ones who didn't live nearby. Once I tried decorating cookies, I didn't look back! Decorating with royal icing allowed me to combine my love of baking with my artistic abilities (drawing and painting were my other hobbies growing up), and with the right packaging, I could ship them anywhere.

Fifteen years later, I have a home studio where I create cookie decorating video tutorials to share with the world.

Over the years, I've created hundreds of cookie designs—and the ideas somehow keep coming! I have moments where I worry I'll never be able to come up with another cookie design, but the moment passes and I have another spark of inspiration.

My cookie ideas come from everywhere. I've created cookies that are inspired by teacups, my kids' toys, patterns on fabric and wallpaper, costumes in TV shows, and even my nail polish.

I keep a list of cookie ideas on my phone and I have a photo album of inspirational pictures and screenshots for future cookies. When I have a creative block, the list and the photo album are the first places I go for inspiration. I've learned, though, that I can't force the ideas to flow. I create my best work when I'm feeling truly inspired. I hope this book can do that for you!

If you're new to royal icing, start with Chapter 1 to learn the ins and outs of decorating with this versatile (yet sometimes finicky) medium. Once you've learned the basics, you can jump around the book to try out different projects.

The designs in this book come with step-by-step instructions and are meant to be recreated by you so you can learn to decorate cookies. As you get more comfortable with decorating, I encourage you to combine these techniques and designs to create your own unique works of edible art. Most importantly, have fun!

Amber Spiegel
Kingston, New York
January 2022

COOKIE
DECORATING
BASICS

TOOLS & EQUIPMENT

When I first started decorating cookies, I purchased many of my supplies from a craft store, but it was still difficult to get specialty products, like edible luster dust. These days, many specialty cake and cookie decorating supply stores exist online, making it much easier to get what I need. To successfully make the cookies in this book, you'll need the following tools and equipment.

STAND MIXER

Since I became a cookie decorator, the stand mixer has become one of my best friends in the kitchen. It's sturdy enough to handle thick royal icing and cookie dough, and the paddle attachment incorporates just enough air without overmixing.

ROLLING PIN

When rolling cookie dough, I use a rolling pin with built-in ¼-inch (0.65cm) guides so my cookies are all the same thickness.

BAKING SHEETS

I use aluminum baking sheets to bake my cookies. These can get pricey if you purchase them new, so check local restaurant supply sales to purchase used baking sheets.

PARCHMENT PAPER

Parchment paper is a great nonstick liner for baking sheets. You can purchase it already cut into rectangles that will fit perfectly on full-size or half-size baking sheets.

PERFORATED BAKING MAT

This is an even better liner than parchment paper—but a little more of an investment. The perforations in the silicone allow air to flow under the mat, baking the cookies evenly and just about perfectly flat.

SPATULAS & SCRAPERS

Some other tools I use for cookie dough and icing are a rubber spatula, a flexible bowl scraper, and small metal spatulas for mixing icing colors.

SCRIBE TOOL

This is probably the most versatile utensil in cookie decorating. With this tool, you can shape and smooth icing, draw guides on a cookie, and fix mistakes—to name a few uses.

DECORATING BAGS, TIPS & COUPLERS

Using decorating tips gives me more control over the icing than tipless decorating bags. In this book, I refer to decorating bags that use couplers and tips as 12-inch (30.5cm) decorating bags. I do use tipless decorating bags for some projects, like when I need just a small amount of icing or if I don't need to be precise when applying it. A tipless decorating bag is made of thin plastic and creates a round hole when you cut an opening in the tip. Cutting a hole in a standard 12-inch (30.5cm) decorating bag will create more of a flat opening because of the thick seam.

I recommend decorating tips from Wilton and the ones I use most often are 1, 2, and 3, which are round tips for flooding and piping details and borders. I also use the following tips:

- **Petal tips:** These have a wide end and a narrow end, and they're used for piping roses and other flowers on a flower nail.

- **Leaf tips:** These have a V shape and they can form a leaf with a vein down the center.

- **Star tips:** These can be used for piping individual stars, but I like to use them to create shell borders.

I use couplers with decorating tips so I can easily switch from one tip to another. Couplers also allow me to remove a clog from a tip without having to empty the icing out of the bag.

Some projects in this book might need more than one tip (such as three #1 tips), so tips are a good investment to make.

BAG CLOSURES
To keep the icing from spilling out of the top of the bag while I'm decorating, I use a bag tie, rubber band, or bag clip.

BRUSHES
There are several different brushes I use for painting on royal icing and for creating textures. The ones I use most often are round brushes for painting large areas and applying dry luster dust, fine tip brushes for small details, and stiff brushes for texturing. My favorites are from Wilton, NY Cake, and Sweet Sticks.

GETTING STARTED WITH COOKIE DECORATING

Making beautiful-looking cookies is a result of practice, patience, and perseverance. When people bite into your cookies, they should enjoy the flavors of the decorative items but also the cookie underneath. The following information will help you create a stable but delicious cookie base for your decorations.

CREATING AN EDIBLE CANVAS

It's important to me that my cookies taste as good as they look. When I first started decorating cookies, they looked beautiful, but they weren't very pleasant to eat. I was using a recipe that had zero spread, which was great for perfectly straight edges but not so great for eating, especially after the cookies sat out for 1 or 2 days while the icing dried! After doing some experimenting, I came up with my Orange, Vanilla & Cardamom recipe (on page 16), which is now the recipe I use most often when making decorated cookies. This recipe has a soft bite, but it's sturdy enough to be shipped across the country (and even around the world!).

I'm okay with my cookies spreading a bit because I know that spreading means the cookie will have a softer bite than one that doesn't spread at all. But if your cookies are spreading more than ¼ inch (0.65cm) past the size of the cookie cutter you used to cut them or if your cookies are becoming misshapen in the oven, the following offers some things you can do to help minimize these issues.

LIMIT THE MIXING TIME.

When creaming the butter and sugar, use a medium speed for the minimum amount of time it takes to create a smooth mixture that's light in color (about 2 minutes).

Good cookie

Bad cookie

Overmixing can incorporate too much air into the dough, leading to the cookies puffing and spreading in the oven.

KEEP THE DOUGH COLD.
The recipes in this book have instructions for chilling the dough. This will help the cookies keep their shape when baking.

REST THE DOUGH.
After you roll out the dough, refrigerate the dough for the amount of time noted in each recipe. This will prevent the cookies from shrinking or warping in the oven.

LIMIT THE SPACING FOR THE CUTOUTS.
When cutting cookies from the dough, space the cutouts as close together as possible to minimize the dough scraps. The more the dough is re-rolled, the higher the chances of getting air bubbles or tough, misshapen cookies.

HANDLING LARGE QUANTITIES OF COOKIES
To make decorating cookies a bit easier, I like to break up the process into smaller steps over a few days.

The cookie dough can be made up to 3 months in advance and stored in the freezer. When I have a lot of cookies to make, I like to make my dough in advance, roll out the sheets of dough, cut the cookies, wrap them, and freeze them raw. When it's time to start decorating, I bake the cookies in batches (right from the freezer—no thawing necessary), only baking as many as I can comfortably decorate in one day.

Once the icing is dry, the cookies can be stored for up to 4 weeks at room temperature (as outlined below). Breaking the process up into steps allows me to finish a couple trays of cookies, wrap them, and get them out of the way while I work on the next batch. It makes it much less overwhelming when there are lots of cookies to make.

STORING & SHIPPING DECORATED COOKIES

Once you've baked your cookies, ice them the same day if possible. Otherwise, store the baked cookies in an airtight container at room temperature for 1 to 2 days.

After you've finished decorating your cookies and the icing is completely dry, store them in an airtight container for up to 1 week at room temperature. If you want them to last longer, wrap them individually in cellophane bags and heat-seal them to keep the cookies tasting fresh for up to 4 weeks at room temperature. You can also place the individually wrapped cookies into an airtight container and freeze them for up to 3 months. Allow the cookies to reach room temperature before removing them from the container. Cookies don't do well in the fridge, so always keep them at room temperature or in the freezer.

Shipping cookies is a great way to share your edible art with friends and family (and customers) around the world. The cookie recipes in this book are sturdy enough to make the trip as long as you package them carefully. Wrap the cookies in tissue paper or bubble wrap after they've been wrapped in cellophane bags—the same way you'd wrap a fragile dish. Layer the wrapped cookies in a gift box and add more tissue paper to fill any extra space. Give the box a little shake to make sure the cookies aren't moving around too much inside the box. Place the gift box into a shipping box and fill the space with craft paper. Another little shake makes sure they're not moving around inside the shipping box—and then they're good to go!

ORANGE, VANILLA & CARDAMOM COOKIES

I've been using this recipe for more than a decade to create my blank cookie canvases. These flavorful cookies are perfect for decorating with royal icing! They're crispy on the edges and chewy on the inside, and the agave syrup helps preserve the soft texture even when they need to sit out for 1 to 2 days while your decorations dry. This yields about 36 cookies (3 inches [7.5cm] in diameter).

4 cups (575g) all-purpose flour, plus more for dusting

1 tsp (4g) baking powder

1 tsp (2g) ground cardamom

1 tsp (5g) kosher salt

1 cup (226g) unsalted butter, softened

1¾ cups (350g) granulated sugar

¼ cup (59ml) agave syrup

zest from a large orange (3.5g)

1 tsp (5ml) vanilla bean paste or 1 vanilla bean, scraped

2 large eggs, room temperature

2 to 3 tbsp (30 to 45ml) whole milk, as needed

1. Sift the flour, baking powder, cardamom, and salt into a medium bowl. Whisk to combine.

2. Add the butter and sugar to the bowl of a stand mixer fitted with the paddle attachment. Mix on medium speed until light and fluffy, about 2 minutes. Stop the mixer and scrape down the bowl and paddle with a rubber spatula as needed.

3. Add the agave syrup, orange zest, and vanilla bean paste or seeds. Mix on low speed until well blended, about 1 minute.

4. Add 1 egg and mix on low speed until well blended. Stop the mixer and scrape the bowl. Add the remaining egg and mix on low speed until well blended.

5. Add the dry ingredients to the wet ingredients. Mix on low speed until everything is incorporated and the dough starts to pull away from the sides of the bowl, about 30 to 60 seconds. The dough should be soft and somewhat sticky but not so sticky it's difficult to handle. If the dough feels too soft, add flour until it stiffens up (about 2 tablespoons at a time). If the dough is very dry and crumbly, add 2 to 3 tablespoons of milk to soften it.

6. Halve the dough and shape each half into a 1-inch-thick (2.5cm) rectangle. Tightly wrap in plastic wrap and refrigerate for 1 hour.

7. Roll out the dough on a floured surface to just under ¼ inch (0.65cm) and chill the sheets for 30 minutes or until firm. Cut out the desired shapes and place them on baking sheets lined with parchment paper. If the cookies are soft, refrigerate them for 15 minutes or until they're firm.

8. Preheat the oven to 350°F (175°C). Transfer the cookies to room temperature baking sheets lined with parchment paper.

9. Place the sheets in the oven and bake the cookies for 10 to 12 minutes or until the edges are light golden brown. Rotate the baking sheets halfway through the baking time.

10. Remove the sheets from the oven and allow the cookies to cool completely.

These cookies will spread slightly while baking. If they spread more than ¼ inch (0.65cm) larger than the cookie cutter, you can make some adjustments by following my tips on page 33.

WHAT IS ROYAL ICING?

If the cookie is the canvas, royal icing is the paint. It's incredibly versatile, allowing cookie artists to make everything from perfectly smooth inlaid designs to intricate 3-dimensional creations. The following will help you make the right consistency of royal icing for the kinds of cookies you want to decorate.

MAKING ROYAL ICING

Royal icing is made by combining confectioners' sugar, egg whites, water, and flavoring. The egg whites can be fresh or in powdered form. I prefer to make my royal icing with meringue powder (dried egg whites), but I've also included a recipe to make it with fresh egg whites (page 36).

Whether it's fresh or powdered, egg whites are what makes royal icing dry hard. You can layer the icing and create all kinds of textures, which is what I love most about it. It's also great for shipping because you don't have to worry about the decorations getting squished inside the box.

ROYAL ICING CONSISTENCIES

Getting the right consistency is one of the most challenging aspects of working with royal icing. This is something that comes with practice, so don't get discouraged if it doesn't come out exactly how you planned right away. There are 3 consistencies I use most often for decorating cookies.

STIFF CONSISTENCY

The royal icing recipes in this book use stiff consistency icing. After you mix the ingredients, the icing holds a stiff peak and has a dull finish. It should be very thick and dense rather than light and fluffy. (Fluffy, overmixed icing can lead to problems when you're decorating cookies. See page 33 for more on overmixed icing.) You can use stiff consistency icing for 3-dimensional roses, brush embroidery, borders, and any decoration that needs to hold its shape.

MEDIUM CONSISTENCY

Medium consistency icing holds a soft peak and has a slightly shinier finish than stiff consistency. This is also known as "piping consistency." It's great for piping lettering, filigree, borders, and small details. Medium consistency icing is thin enough to easily come out of a small tip but not so thin it loses its shape. To create medium consistency icing, start with stiff consistency and add ½ teaspoon of water per cup of icing until it holds a soft peak.

TIPS FOR THE IDEAL CONSISTENCY

Getting the right consistency for your icing takes practice and patience. The following tips should help ensure you get the consistency you need.

Using meringue powder: I prefer to use meringue powder because I can be sure to get a consistent result every time, as opposed to egg whites, which can vary in size and water content. I also like that meringue powder is shelf-stable, so I don't have to worry about it going bad before I can use it.

Thickening the icing: If your stiff consistency icing isn't holding a peak, add more confectioners' sugar and meringue powder. I keep a batch of the mixed dry ingredients in an airtight container, and if I need to thicken my icing, I add some of this mixture. To thicken medium or flood consistency, add a small scoop of stiff consistency icing.

Experimenting: See pages 36–41 for royal icing flavor variations and other types of frosting recipes to try with the techniques in this book.

FLOOD CONSISTENCY

Flood consistency icing creates a perfectly smooth base coat on a cookie. It's also used for the wet-on-wet technique, which is done by piping one or more colors of icing on the cookie while the base layer of icing is still wet.

To make flood consistency icing, start with medium consistency or stiff consistency and stir in ½ to 1 teaspoon of water per cup of icing until it reaches a 15- to 20-second count. This means it will take 15 to 20 seconds for the surface of the icing to become smooth.

To test the icing consistency, take a scoop of icing out of the bowl and drop it back in. It should take between 15 and 20 seconds to smooth out on its own. If the icing smooths out faster than 15 seconds, it's too thin and it will run off the edges of a cookie. Add a small scoop of stiff consistency icing to thicken it and test the consistency again.

Keep in mind that adding food coloring will affect your icing consistency, so be sure to test the consistency again after adding the food coloring.

VANILLA ROYAL ICING
WITH MERINGUE POWDER

This is my go-to recipe when decorating cookies. Royal icing is a very basic recipe made with just a few ingredients, but the trick is in the technique. Make sure to not overmix the icing and add the water gradually, as laid out in the instructions. This yields enough icing to decorate about 48 (3-inch [7.5cm]) cookies.

7½ cups (907g) confectioners' sugar

½ cup plus 2 tbsp (104g) meringue powder

⅛ tsp (0.10g) kosher salt

½ cup (118ml) to ¾ cup (177ml) room temperature water, plus more for thinning

1 tsp (5ml) pure vanilla extract

1. Sift the confectioners' sugar, meringue powder, and salt into the bowl of a stand mixer.

2. Fit the mixer with the paddle attachment. Mix on low speed until combined, about 30 seconds.

3. Add ½ cup (118mL) of water and the vanilla extract. Mix on low speed until combined. If the mixture is dry and crumbly, add more water 1 tablespoon at a time until the ingredients are saturated. Be careful not to add too much water. At this point, the icing should be wet but not dripping off the paddle attachment. See the tip on page 33 to fix the icing if you've added too much water.

4. Stop the mixer and scrape the bowl. Resume the mixer on speed 2 (low speed) for 3 to 4 minutes. It's very important you don't overmix the icing. The icing should hold a stiff peak and have a dull finish. See pages 18–19 for instructions on how to thin the icing to different consistencies.

5. Store the icing in an airtight container in the fridge for up to 10 days or in the freezer for up to 3 months.

MAKING COLORED ROYAL ICING

Just between you and me, coloring royal icing is my least favorite part of the whole cookie decorating process. I want to get to the fun part as quickly as possible, but it can take me an hour or more to get all the colors ready for a project. I make things a little easier on myself by prepping my colors 1 to 2 days ahead of time. That way, when it's time to decorate the cookies, I can jump right in!

WHAT TO USE TO MAKE COLORED ICING

When coloring royal icing, use concentrated gel or liquid gel colors. If you use the watery liquids you find in grocery stores, you'll end up adding an entire bottle of food coloring to get the shade you want. My favorite gel colors brands are Chefmaster and Wilton Color Right.

I make my colors by eye, but if you're not sure how much blue to add to a certain shade of green to make it look teal green, color wheels or color charts are very helpful. There are tons of resources online for mixing colors.

HOW TO MAKE COLORED ICING

The projects in this book call for a certain number of drops of food coloring, but you might need more or less depending on the brand of color you're using. You can adjust the color by adding more food coloring to darken the shade or by adding more white icing to lighten it. Keep in mind that it's easier to darken a shade than to lighten it, so err on the side of adding too little food coloring than adding too much.

To color royal icing, stir a small amount of food coloring into the icing and add more as you need it. Keep in mind that icing colors will darken over several hours, so make your icing 1 to 2 shades lighter than what you want to see on your cookie. This is especially important when making dark colors, like black or red. If you try to make your colors super dark right away, you'll end up putting too much food coloring in your icing, which can lead to color bleed. (See page 33 for more.) When creating black icing, I make a dark shade of gray and let it sit for a few hours or overnight. Then the icing is ready for me by the time I want to decorate my cookies.

You can add food coloring to your icing before, during, or after thinning it to the consistency you need. Gel food coloring can thicken your icing a bit, so you might need to add a few drops of water to thin it back down to flood consistency after you add the color.

No matter how precise we are with adding color to icing, it's nearly impossible to recreate an icing color a second time. Make enough of one color for the whole project, plus a little extra just in case. On the other hand, even if you do end up having to match a color and it's a little bit off, it's very unlikely anyone will notice.

SMELL YOUR COLORS!

If you've decorated cookies before, you might have had the unpleasant experience of your black or red icing tasting somewhat like a permanent marker. Some gel colors have a very strong taste, so it's a good idea to smell it (or even taste it) before you add it to your icing. The brands of food coloring I recommend in this chapter haven't caused this problem in my experience.

USING A DECORATING BAG

Before you fill your decorating bag, you need to decide which type of bag you're going to use for your project. Do you need decorating tips? Can you make do with tipless bags? A project might call for tipped and tipless bags, but you can complete most of the projects in this book with whatever you're most comfortable using.

HOW TO FILL
A DECORATING BAG

The following steps detail how to prepare a tipped decorating bag for filling as well as how to fill it with icing. If you're using a tipless decorating bag, jump to step 6.

1. Remove the coupler ring from the coupler. Insert the coupler base tip side down into the bag, pushing the coupler base into the tip of the bag until the plastic is taut around the base.

2. Use a pair of scissors to make a mark on the thread of the coupler base that's closest to the tip of the bag.

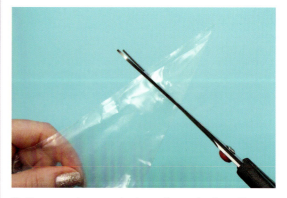

3. Remove the coupler base from the bag. Trim the bag at the scissors mark.

4. Push the coupler back into the tip of the bag and place the decorating tip over it. Place the coupler ring on the coupler base and screw the ring until tight.

6. Pull down the sides of the bag around your hand to create a well in the bag. Fill the bag with a few scoops of icing, making sure not to overfill. It's so much easier to control the icing placement when the bag is only filled halfway.

5. Twist the bag right above the coupler base and push it into the coupler base to prevent the icing from coming out of the icing tip when you fill the bag with icing.

7. Secure the top of the bag with a rubber band, bag tie, or clip. Whatever you're using, make sure to keep it as close to the top of the bag as possible rather than right up against the icing. This gives you room to hold the bag comfortably when you're decorating your cookies.

HOW TO FIX A LOOSE TIP

If your decorating tip is wiggling even though your coupler is screwed on tightly, remove the coupler ring and check that there's no plastic from the bag in the way of the threads. If that's not the issue, it could be you're using pieces from 2 different couplers that don't go together. (When you start amassing a collection of couplers, they tend to get mixed up!) Try using another coupler ring to attach to the coupler base.

HOW TO FLOOD A COOKIE

The flooding technique is the best way to create a smooth icing surface on your cookies. When I teach cookie decorating classes, I give my students reusable plastic cookies to flood over and over again so they have plenty of practice before we move on to more advanced decorating techniques. You might be surprised by how much your flooding technique can improve in the span of just 30 minutes. I've seen it with my own eyes from students who've never decorated a cookie before! The following steps will help you practice and perfect your flooding skills.

1. Hold a filled decorating bag about halfway down. You want to work with just a handful of icing at a time. The rest of the icing will be behind your hand, held in by a bag tie. It's helpful to twist the bag just a bit where it sits in the crook of your thumb. This will make it so you don't have to squeeze too hard when flooding the cookie. If you made a plug in the tip of your bag before filling it, make sure to pull the tip to release the plug. If you're using a tipless bag, trim a very small hole in the tip.

2. Rest your forearm on a table to steady your hand as you decorate. Place your other hand on top of your decorating hand for more support.

3. Gently squeeze the bag and outline the cookie, leaving about ¼ inch (0.65cm) around the edge. Don't worry about creating a perfect circle because you'll shape it later with the scribe tool.

4. Increase the pressure as you move toward the center of the cookie. You want to have a mound of icing on the cookie. If you don't put enough icing on the cookie, it will end up being bumpy. On the other hand, if you put too much icing, it will run off the edges. Getting the right amount of icing on the cookie comes with practice.

5. Hold the scribe tool like a pencil and keep it at around 7 o'clock on the cookie. While turning the cookie clockwise, move the scribe tool in a circular counterclockwise motion, pushing the icing toward the edge of the cookie. (If you're left-handed, hold the scribe tool at around 5 o'clock and do the opposite motions.) This will help create a nice round shape.

6. When you're done, there should be about ⅛ inch (3mm) of space all the way around.

TIPS FOR THE BEST FLOODING

Why not use a stiff outline? My flooding technique doesn't require piping an outline with a stiffer consistency of icing. I use flood consistency icing for outlining and flooding because I don't want to have to mix 2 colors of the same consistency. Also, I find it very difficult to pipe a perfect circle and this technique allows me to avoid that. The other reason I use only flood consistency for this technique is because the edges are perfectly smooth with no visible outline.

Why leave space around the edge of a cookie? I like to leave a little space around the edge of a cookie to have room for a border. Even if I'm not adding a border, I like the dimension it adds with having a little bit of the cookie showing. Another benefit of leaving room around the edge is that the icing has space to expand a bit without flowing over the side of the cookie.

How can I adjust the icing consistency? If you're flooding your cookie and the icing is running off the edge or it's difficult to spread the icing with the scribe tool, you might have to empty the decorating bag and adjust the consistency. Even after 15 years of decorating cookies, I still have days when my icing consistency is off!

HOW TO PIPE BORDERS

Different types of borders call for different consistencies of icing. I use stiff consistency icing most often for my bead borders, but when I'm piping a very small bead, I prefer to use medium consistency because it's easier to squeeze out of a small decorating tip. The following borders can be piped with a tipless bag, although I prefer using tips because they give me a smoother shape.

SINGLE-BEAD BORDER

Use stiff or medium consistency icing and a round tip for the decorating bag for this border. Hold the tip at a 45° angle against the cookie. Squeeze the decorating bag to form a bead and then release the pressure before moving the tip away from the bead while pressing the tip against the cookie to end the bead. There should be a small tail—shaped like a teardrop. Begin the next bead so it just covers the tail of the previous bead. Continue this all the way around, moving the cookie as you pipe. Once you get the hang of this, the process should feel like a fluid, wavelike motion. The last bead is always a little tricky because the last space can be a little too small or too big. Do your best to fit one last bead in the space and then use your scribe tool or a dry brush to shape the bead to look like the rest.

DOUBLE-BEAD BORDER

Use stiff or medium consistency icing and a round tip for the decorating bag for this border. Hold the tip at a 45° angle against the cookie. Squeeze the decorating bag to form a bead and then release the pressure before moving the tip away from the bead while pressing the tip against the cookie to end the bead. There should be a small tail—shaped like a teardrop. Begin the next bead so it just covers the tail of the bead before it, angling the tip so the 2 beads are facing slightly away from each other. Continue this all the way around, moving the cookie as you pipe.

SINGLE-SHELL & DOUBLE-SHELL BORDERS

Use stiff consistency icing and a star tip for the decorating bag for these borders. This technique is the same as the bead borders. While you can choose between medium and stiff consistency icing for the bead borders, shell borders require stiff consistency icing to hold the small ridges.

REVERSE SHELL BORDER

Use stiff consistency icing and a star tip for the decorating bag for this border. Hold the tip straight up and down, and squeeze the bag to form a swirl, with the head of the swirl facing either to the left or right. Just like when piping a shell or a bead, squeeze the bag to let the icing build up and then

release the pressure as you move the tip away, forming a tail. Start the next swirl so it just covers the tail of the swirl before it. This swirl will be facing in the opposite direction from the first one. Continue this all the way around, with each swirl facing away from each other.

DOT BORDER

Use stiff, medium, or flood consistency icing for this border. Use a round tip for the decorating bag or use a tipless decorating bag. This border is the most forgiving, making it a great starting border for beginners. You can use any consistency you like, but keep in mind that if you're using flood consistency icing, you'll have to leave space between each dot. Otherwise, they'll blend together and you'll lose the definition of the border. Hold the decorating bag straight up and down, hovering just above the cookie. Gently squeeze the decorating bag to form a bead and release the pressure before moving away from the bead. If you're using medium or stiff consistency icing, swirl the tip on the surface of the bead before pulling away to avoid creating a peak.

PAINTING ON ROYAL ICING

If you're like me, you don't enjoy mixing icing colors. Painting on royal icing is a great way to avoid that! You can also use this technique to create effects you can't get with piped icing, like ombre and watercolor. The following are what you can use to paint on royal icing.

FOOD COLORING

The type of color you choose to paint on your cookies will depend on the look you want to achieve. To create a watercolor effect on royal icing, use gel, liquid gel, or airbrush food coloring. If you want your paint to be opaque, use matte edible dust (also called "petal dust"). I use a combination of gel and matte dust for painting.

LUSTER DUST OR PEARL DUST

These edible dusts can be used dry for a light sheen or with liquid for a more intense shine. When painting with gold luster dust, start with a golden brown icing base for the best result. Use a gray, black, or blue base for silver luster dust. It's always good to experiment with base colors to see what looks best for your project.

When painting on royal icing, the food coloring (gel or dust) works best when it's mixed with vodka or grain alcohol to dilute it. You can also use extracts as long as they're alcohol based. Alcohol evaporates very quickly, which means it won't dissolve the icing as you paint. If your icing is still dissolving even though you're using alcohol, see the royal icing troubleshooting on page 33.

Place a small amount of food coloring on a paint palette or in a small dish and add a few drops of alcohol to dilute it. Use more or less liquid depending on how light or dark you want your colors to be. A brush dipped in alcohol can be used to blend colors to create an ombre effect.

TIPS FOR THE BEST PAINTINGS

If you wish to avoid alcohol, you can substitute water when painting on royal icing. Keep in mind that this runs the risk of dissolving the icing as you paint, so try to paint quickly and don't hold your brush in one spot for too long.

Before you use luster dust or petal dust, check the label to make sure it's edible. Some dusts have "nontoxic" labels, which means it won't harm you, but it's not been approved for consumption.

HOW TO PIPE ROSES

You can pipe these roses in advance. Once dry, they'll last several months in an airtight container at room temperature. You'll need parchment or wax paper squares and a flower nail for piping roses.

1. Hold the decorating tip with the wide end down and the narrow end facing up and angled slightly inward.

2. Pipe a small mound of icing shaped like a cone, with the narrow end of the cone at the top. This will be the flower center.

3. Touch the decorating tip to the flower center to anchor the next layer of icing. Squeeze the bag while turning the flower nail to wrap the icing all the way around the flower center. This should look like a tight rosebud.

4. Touch the decorating tip to the rosebud to anchor the first petal. Squeeze the bag and create an arc with the icing while turning the flower nail to make a petal. Finish the petal with a quick flicking motion.

5. Touch the decorating tip to the first petal to anchor the next petal. The second petal should slightly overlap the first. Squeeze the bag and create an arc with the icing while turning the flower nail. Finish the petal with a quick flicking motion.

6. Touch the decorating tip to the first petal to anchor the third petal. The third petal should slightly overlap the second. Squeeze the bag and create an arc with the icing while turning the flower nail, ending the third petal behind the first one. Finish the petal with a quick flicking motion. For the outer layer, repeat the process for making the previous 3 petals, but pipe 5 petals this time.

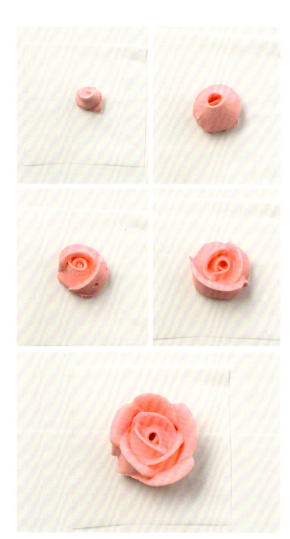

TROUBLESHOOTING

Few things are more frustrating than spending hours on a set of cookies only to come back the next day and see that the colors have bled, the icing is bumpy (it was so smooth when it was flooded!), or the icing hasn't dried at all. While most of these issues can't be remedied once they've occurred, the following tips will help prevent them from happening in the first place.

DON'T OVERMIX ICING.

Follow the instructions in the Vanilla Royal Icing recipe (page 20) and only mix the icing for 3 to 4 minutes on low speed (speed 2 on a stand mixer). Overmixed icing can contribute to color bleed; butter bleed (blotchy or yellowing icing); air bubbles; dull, sandy, or spongy icing; and icing not drying thoroughly.

DON'T ADD TOO MUCH WATER.

Watery icing can lead to color bleed, butter bleed, air bubbles, and very fragile icing. Test your icing consistency to make sure it's between the 15- to 20-second count. See pages 18–19 for more on icing consistencies.

DON'T ADD TOO MUCH FOOD COLORING.

When making dark colors, start a few hours or a day ahead of time so the colors have time to darken on their own. Adding too much color can lead to color bleed; dull, sandy, or spongy icing; and icing not drying thoroughly.

OTHER PROBLEMS WITH ROYAL ICING

If the following issues occur, try not to worry too much. You can always cover them up with more decorations! And remember, even though these flaws might be noticeable to you, the recipient will only see a beautiful set of cookies.

Craters: This is one of the most common problems in cookie decorating aside from color bleed. When icing very small areas on a cookie, the icing tends to dip or even completely cave in, leaving a hole. To prevent this, try using a slightly thicker icing consistency. You can also create a support for the icing by piping a small dot or line in the area that needs to be filled in. Let the icing crust over and then flood on top of it. The dot or line you piped first will help prevent the icing from caving in.

Clogged tips or curling icing: Sifting the confectioners' sugar usually isn't necessary because the sugar contains cornstarch, which helps prevent clumping. But if your tips are constantly clogged, it might be a good idea to sift the confectioners' sugar next time you make the icing. Or once the icing is made, you can strain it through a nylon stocking to remove any little clumps. Sometimes, a partial clog in a tip can cause the icing to curl as it comes out. If you've already sifted the confectioners' sugar or strained your icing and it's still happening, the issue might be a defect inside the tip or you could be squeezing the decorating bag too hard as you pipe.

ICING & FROSTING RECIPES

VANILLA ROYAL ICING
WITH FRESH EGG WHITES

No meringue powder on hand? No problem! You can use fresh egg whites to make royal icing. It's a little more difficult to control the moisture content when using fresh egg whites, but this recipe is the next best thing for when you don't have meringue powder in the kitchen. This yields enough icing to decorate about 24 cookies (3 inches [7.5cm] in diameter).

4 cups (454g) confectioners' sugar

¼ cup (30g) cornstarch

1 tsp (4g) cream of tartar

pinch of Morton's kosher salt

½ cup (118ml) pasteurized egg whites (3 to 4 large egg whites), room temperature

1 tsp (5ml) pure vanilla extract

1. Sift the confectioners' sugar, cornstarch, cream of tartar, and salt into the bowl of a stand mixer. Fit the mixer with the paddle attachment. Mix on low speed until combined, about 30 seconds.

2. Add the egg whites and vanilla extract. Continue to mix on low speed until combined. If the mixture is dry and crumbly, add more egg whites 1 tablespoon at a time until the ingredients are saturated. Be careful not to add too much liquid. At this point, the icing should be wet but not dripping off the attachment.

3. Stop the mixer and scrape the bowl. Resume the mixer on speed 2 (low speed) for 3 to 4 minutes. It's very important you don't overmix the icing. The icing should hold a stiff peak and have a dull finish. (See page 19 for instructions on how to thin the icing to different consistencies.)

4. Transfer the icing to an airtight container. Store in the fridge for up to 5 days or in the freezer for up to 3 months.

CHOCOLATE ROYAL ICING

Just like with vanilla royal icing, you can use this delicious chocolate royal icing for a variety of cookie decorating techniques—from flooding cookies to piping roses. This yields enough icing to decorate about 24 cookies (3 inches [7.5cm] in diameter).

4 cups (454g) confectioners' sugar

¼ cup plus 1 tbsp (52g) meringue powder

1 cup (85g) cocoa powder

pinch of Morton's kosher salt

½ cup (118ml) to ¾ cup (177ml) room temperature water, plus more for thinning

1 tsp (5ml) pure vanilla extract

1. Sift the confectioners' sugar, meringue powder, cocoa powder, and salt into the bowl of a stand mixer. Fit the mixer with the paddle attachment. Mix the ingredients on low speed until combined, about 30 seconds.

2. Add the ½ cup (118ml) of water and vanilla extract. Mix on low speed until combined. If the mixture is dry and crumbly, add more water 1 tablespoon at a time until the ingredients are saturated. Be careful not to add too much water. At this point, the icing should be wet but not dripping off the attachment. (See the tip on page 33 to fix the icing if you've added too much water.)

3. Stop the mixer and scrape the bowl. Resume the mixer on speed 2 (low speed) for 3 to 4 minutes. It's very important you don't overmix the icing. The icing should hold a stiff peak and have a dull finish. (See page 19 for instructions on how to thin the icing to different consistencies.)

4. Transfer the icing to an airtight container. Store in the fridge for up to 10 days or in the freezer for up to 3 months.

This chocolate royal icing tastes fantastic, but keep in mind that because it contains fat from the cocoa powder, it's more susceptible to fragility, color bleed, and other issues mentioned on page 33.

COFFEE ROYAL ICING

Being a coffee drinker, I was very excited to try adding instant coffee to my royal icing recipe. The natural light brown color of this coffee-flavored icing is perfect for making latte art cookies (pages 158–159). This yields enough icing to decorate about 24 cookies (3 inches [7.5cm] in diameter).

1 tbsp (6g) instant coffee

1 tbsp (15ml) hot water

4 cups (454g) confectioners' sugar

¼ cup plus 1 tbsp (52g) meringue powder

pinch of Morton's kosher salt

⅓ cup (79ml) to ½ cup (118ml) room temperature water, plus more for thinning

1 tsp (5ml) pure vanilla extract

1. In a small dish, dissolve the instant coffee in 1 tablespoon of hot water. Set aside.

2. Sift the confectioners' sugar, meringue powder, and salt into the bowl of a stand mixer. Fit the mixer with the paddle attachment. Mix the ingredients on low speed until combined, about 30 seconds.

3. Add the ⅓ cup (79ml) of water, dissolved instant coffee, and vanilla extract. Mix on low speed until combined. If the mixture is dry and crumbly, add more water 1 tablespoon at a time until the ingredients are saturated. Be careful not to add too much water. At this point, the icing should be wet but not dripping off the paddle attachment. (See the tip on page 33 to fix the icing if you've added too much water.)

4. Stop the mixer and scrape the bowl. Resume the mixer on speed 2 (low speed) for 3 to 4 minutes. It's very important you don't overmix the icing. The icing should hold a stiff peak and have a dull finish. (See page 19 for instructions on how to thin the icing to different consistencies.)

5. Transfer the icing to an airtight container. Store in the fridge for up to 10 days or in the freezer for up to 3 months.

Just like Chocolate Royal Icing (page 37), this royal icing contains fat from the instant coffee in the recipe, making it more susceptible to fragility, color bleed, and other issues mentioned on page 33.

VANILLA BUTTERCREAM FROSTING

The consistency of this frosting is perfect for making piped roses and shell borders. (See the Birthday Cake cookies on pages 78–81!) You can also use this sweet and creamy frosting to decorate your favorite cake and cupcake recipes. This yields enough frosting for about 24 cookies (3 inches [7.5cm] in diameter).

1 cup (226g) unsalted butter, softened

4 cups (454g) confectioners' sugar, divided

¼ tsp (0.25g) Morton's kosher salt

1 tbsp (15ml) pure vanilla extract

2 to 4 tbsp (30 to 60ml) whole milk, slightly warm

1. Add the butter to the bowl of a stand mixer fitted with the paddle attachment. Mix on medium speed until smooth, about 30 seconds.

2. Add 1 cup of confectioners' sugar and the salt. Blend on low speed until combined. Continue to add the confectioners' sugar 1 cup at a time, blending between each addition.

3. Add the vanilla extract and 2 tablespoons of milk. Mix on low speed until combined. If the frosting is very stiff, add more milk 1 tablespoon at a time until the frosting is smooth but still holds a stiff peak.

4. Mix on high speed until light and fluffy, about 1 minute.

5. Transfer the frosting to an airtight container and store in the fridge for up to 1 week. Allow the frosting to come to room temperature and mix it on high speed for 1 minute before using.

CHOCOLATE BUTTERCREAM FROSTING

If you can resist eating this straight out of the bowl, this delicious chocolate frosting is perfect for piping beautiful roses and shell borders on cookies, cakes, and cupcakes. This yields enough frosting for about 24 cookies (3 inches [7.5cm] in diameter).

4 cups (454g) confectioners' sugar

1 cup (85g) cocoa powder

¼ tsp (0.25g) Morton's kosher salt

1 cup (226g) unsalted butter, softened

2 tsp (10ml) pure vanilla extract

¼ to ½ cup (59 to 118ml) whole milk, slightly warm

1. Sift the confectioners' sugar, cocoa powder, and salt into a large bowl. Whisk to combine.

2. Add the butter in the bowl of a stand mixer fitted with the paddle attachment or to a large bowl if using a hand mixer. Mix on medium speed until smooth, about 30 seconds.

3. Add about half the dry ingredients to the wet ingredients. Blend on low speed until combined. Stop the mixer and scrape the bowl.

4. Add the vanilla extract and ¼ cup of milk. Mix on low speed until combined. Stop the mixer and scrape the bowl.

5. Add the remaining dry ingredients and blend on low speed until combined. Stop the mixer and scrape the bowl. If the frosting is very stiff, add more milk 1 tablespoon at a time until the frosting is smooth but still holds a stiff peak.

6. Mix on high speed until light and fluffy, about 1 minute.

7. Transfer the frosting to an airtight container and store in the fridge for up to 1 week. Allow the frosting to come to room temperature and mix it on high speed for 1 minute before using.

WHIPPED WHITE CHOCOLATE GANACHE

This sweet and creamy combination of just 2 simple ingredients that can be sandwiched between 2 meringue cookies is a dream! You can also use this ganache to top your favorite cookies, cakes, or cupcakes. This yields enough ganache to fill about 50 meringue cookie sandwiches.

1 cup (160g) white chocolate chips
1 cup (237ml) heavy cream

1. Add the white chocolate chips to a medium heatproof, microwaveable bowl.

2. Heat the heavy cream in a small saucepan on the stovetop over medium heat until steaming, stirring occasionally. Remove the saucepan from the stovetop and allow the heavy cream to cool to about 120°F (50°C).

3. Pour the warm heavy cream over the white chocolate chips. Whisk until smooth. If the chips haven't melted in 5 minutes, microwave for 10 seconds and whisk again until smooth.

4. Refrigerate the ganache for at least 2 hours to thicken.

5. Use a stand mixer with the whisk attachment or a hand mixer to whip the ganache on medium speed until it's fluffy, about 1 minute.

6. Transfer the ganache to an airtight container and store in the fridge for up to 1 week. Allow the ganache to come to room temperature and mix on medium speed for 1 minute before using.

Pipe this white chocolate ganache between 2 meringue cookies to create the dreamiest cookie sandwich ever! The Meringue Cookies recipe is on page 53.

COOKIE
RECIPES

VANILLA COOKIES

Flavored with rich vanilla bean paste, these cookies are anything but plain! The addition of agave syrup helps keep the cookies soft, which is the perfect complement to the crispy texture of royal icing. This yields about 36 cookies (3 inches [7.5cm] in diameter).

4 cups (575g) all-purpose flour, plus more for dusting

1 tsp (4g) baking powder

1 tsp (5g) Morton's kosher salt

1 cup (226g) unsalted butter, softened

1¾ cups (350g) granulated sugar

¼ cup (59ml) agave syrup

1 tbsp (15ml) vanilla bean paste or 1 vanilla bean, scraped

2 large eggs, room temperature

2 to 3 tbsp (30 to 45ml) whole milk, as needed

1. Sift the flour, baking powder, and salt into a medium bowl. Whisk to combine.

2. Add the butter and sugar to the bowl of a stand mixer fitted with the paddle attachment. Mix on medium speed until light and fluffy, about 2 minutes. Stop the mixer and scrape the bowl.

3. Add the agave syrup and vanilla bean paste or vanilla bean seeds. Mix on low speed until well blended, about 1 minute.

4. Add 1 egg and mix on low speed until well blended. Stop the mixer and scrape the bowl. Add the remaining egg and mix on low speed until well blended.

5. Add the dry ingredients to the wet ingredients. Mix on low speed until everything is incorporated and the dough starts to pull away from the sides of the bowl, about 30 to 60 seconds. The dough should be soft and somewhat sticky but not so sticky that it's difficult to handle. If the dough feels too soft, add flour until it stiffens (about 2 tablespoons at a time). If the dough is very dry and crumbly, add 2 to 3 tablespoons of milk to soften.

6. Halve the dough and shape each half into a 1-inch-thick (2.5cm) rectangle. Tightly wrap in plastic wrap and refrigerate for 1 hour.

7. Roll out the dough on a floured surface to just under ¼ inch (0.65cm) and chill the sheets for 30 minutes or until firm. Cut out the desired shapes and place them on baking sheets lined with parchment paper. If the cookies are soft, refrigerate for 15 minutes or until firm.

8. Preheat the oven to 350°F (175°C). Transfer the cookies to room temperature baking sheets lined with parchment paper.

9. Place the sheets in the oven and bake the cookies for 10 to 12 minutes or until the edges are light golden brown. Rotate the baking sheets halfway through the baking time. Remove the sheets from the oven and allow the cookies to cool completely.

PUMPKIN SPICE COOKIES

These cookies capture the flavors of my favorite holiday dessert: pumpkin pie!
Top them with any of the icing recipes in this book to create delicious flavor
combinations. This yields about 36 cookies (3 inches [7.5cm] in diameter).

4 cups (575g) all-purpose flour,
plus more for dusting

1 tsp (4g) baking powder

2 tsp (2g) pumpkin spice

1 tsp (5g) Morton's kosher salt

1 cup (226g) unsalted butter,
softened

1 cup (200g) granulated sugar

¾ cup (160g) light brown sugar

½ cup (118ml) canned pumpkin
purée

1 tsp (5ml) pure vanilla extract

2 large eggs, room temperature

2 to 3 tbsp (30 to 45ml) whole
milk, as needed

1. Sift the flour, baking powder, pumpkin spice, and salt into
a medium bowl. Whisk to combine.

2. Add the butter, granulated sugar, and brown sugar to the bowl
of a stand mixer fitted with the paddle attachment. Mix on medium
speed until light and fluffy, about 2 minutes. Stop the mixer and
scrape the bowl.

3. Add the pumpkin purée and vanilla extract. Mix on low speed
until well blended, about 1 minute.

4. Add 1 egg and mix on low speed until well blended. Stop the
mixer and scrape the bowl. Add the remaining egg and mix on low
speed until well blended.

5. Add the dry ingredients to the wet ingredients. Mix on low
speed until everything is incorporated and the dough starts to
pull away from the sides of the bowl, about 30 to 60 seconds.
The dough should be soft and somewhat sticky but not so sticky
that it's difficult to handle. If the dough feels too soft, add flour
until it stiffens (about 2 tablespoons at a time). If the dough is
very dry and crumbly, add 2 to 3 tablespoons of milk to soften.

6. Halve the dough and shape each half into a 1-inch-thick (2.5cm)
rectangle. Tightly wrap in plastic wrap and refrigerate for 1 hour.

7. Roll out the dough on a floured surface to just under ¼ inch
(0.65cm) and chill the sheets for 30 minutes or until firm. Cut out
the desired shapes and place them on baking sheets lined with
parchment paper. If the cookies are soft, refrigerate them for
15 minutes or until firm.

8. Preheat the oven to 350°F (175°C). Transfer the cookies to
room temperature baking sheets lined with parchment paper.

9. Place the sheets in the oven and bake the cookies for 10 to 12
minutes or until the edges are light golden brown. Rotate the
baking sheets halfway through the baking time. Remove the
sheets from the oven and allow the cookies to cool completely.

LEMON & ALMOND COOKIES

These lemon and almond cookies are a fresh take on my original cookie recipe. This is one of my favorite flavor combinations! This yields about 36 cookies (3 inches [7.5cm] in diameter).

4 cups (575g) all-purpose flour, plus more for dusting

1 tsp (4g) baking powder

1 tsp (5g) Morton's kosher salt

1 cup (226g) unsalted butter, softened

1¾ cups (350g) granulated sugar

¼ cup (59ml) agave syrup

2 tsp lemon zest

2 tbsp freshly squeezed lemon juice

2 tsp (10ml) pure vanilla extract

¼ tsp (1.25ml) pure almond extract

2 large eggs, room temperature

2 to 3 tbsp (30 to 45ml) whole milk, as needed

1. Sift the flour, baking powder, and salt into a medium bowl. Whisk to combine.

2. Add the butter and sugar to the bowl of a stand mixer fitted with the paddle attachment. Mix on medium speed until light and fluffy, about 2 minutes. Stop the mixer and scrape the bowl.

3. Add the agave syrup, lemon zest and juice, vanilla extract, and almond extract. Mix on low speed until well blended, about 1 minute.

4. Add 1 egg and mix on low speed until well blended. Stop the mixer and scrape the bowl. Add the remaining egg and mix on low speed until well blended.

5. Add the dry ingredients to the wet ingredients. Mix on low speed until everything is incorporated and the dough starts to pull away from the sides of the bowl, about 30 to 60 seconds. The dough should be soft and somewhat sticky but not so sticky that it's difficult to handle. If the dough feels too soft, add flour until it stiffens (about 2 tablespoons at a time). If the dough is very dry and crumbly, add 2 to 3 tablespoons of milk to soften.

6. Halve the dough and shape each half into a 1-inch-thick (2.5cm) rectangle. Tightly wrap in plastic wrap and refrigerate for 1 hour.

7. Roll out the dough on a floured surface to just under ¼ inch (0.65cm) and chill the sheets for 30 minutes or until firm. Cut out the desired shapes and place them on baking sheets lined with parchment paper. If the cookies are soft, refrigerate them for 15 minutes or until firm.

8. Preheat the oven to 350°F (175°C). Transfer the cookies to room temperature baking sheets lined with parchment paper.

9. Place the sheets in the oven and bake the cookies for 10 to 12 minutes or until the edges are light golden brown. Rotate the baking sheets halfway through the baking time. Remove the sheets from the oven and allow the cookies to cool completely.

LIME & COCONUT COOKIES

Fresh lime zest and toasted coconut come together to create a perfectly delicious canvas for your summer cookie designs. This yields about 36 cookies (3 inches [7.5cm] in diameter).

1 cup (85g) sweetened coconut flakes, toasted

4 cups (575g) all-purpose flour, plus more for dusting

1 tsp (4g) baking powder

1 tsp (5g) Morton's kosher salt

1 cup (226g) unsalted butter, softened

1½ cups (300g) granulated sugar

¼ cup (59ml) agave syrup

1 tsp (5ml) pure vanilla extract

2 tsp lime zest

1 tbsp freshly squeezed lime juice, plus more as needed

2 large eggs, room temperature

1. Add the toasted coconut to a food processor and grind for a few seconds. It's okay if there are a few large pieces left.

2. Sift the flour, baking powder, and salt into a medium bowl. Add the toasted coconut and whisk to combine.

3. Add the butter and sugar to the bowl of a stand mixer fitted with the paddle attachment. Mix on medium speed until light and fluffy, about 2 minutes. Stop the mixer and scrape the bowl.

4. Add the agave syrup, vanilla extract, and lime zest and juice. Mix on low speed until well blended, about 1 minute.

5. Add 1 egg and mix on low speed until well blended. Stop the mixer and scrape the bowl. Add the remaining egg and mix on low speed until well blended.

6. Add the dry ingredients to the wet ingredients. Mix on low speed until everything is incorporated and the dough starts to pull away from the sides of the bowl, about 30 to 60 seconds. The dough should be soft and somewhat sticky but not so sticky that it's difficult to handle. If the dough feels too soft, add flour until it stiffens (about 2 tablespoons at a time). If the dough is very dry and crumbly, add 2 to 3 tablespoons of lime juice to soften.

7. Halve the dough and shape each half into a 1-inch-thick (2.5cm) rectangle. Tightly wrap in plastic wrap and refrigerate for 1 hour.

8. Roll out out the dough on a floured surface to just under ¼ inch (0.65cm) and chill the sheets for 30 minutes or until firm. Cut out the desired shapes and place them on baking sheets lined with parchment paper. If the cookies are soft, refrigerate them for 15 minutes or until firm.

9. Preheat the oven to 350°F (175°C). Transfer the cookies to room temperature baking sheets lined with parchment paper.

10. Place the sheets in the oven and bake the cookies for 10 to 12 minutes or until the edges are light golden brown. Rotate the baking sheets halfway through the baking time. Remove the sheets from the oven and allow the cookies to cool completely.

CHOCOLATE COOKIES

These cutout cookies are deliciously chocolatey, with a little hint of coffee to boost the flavor. I highly recommend you try these chocolate cookies with Coffee Royal Icing (page 38)! This yields about 36 cookies (3 inches [7.5cm] in diameter).

1 tsp (2.5g) instant coffee

1 tbsp (15ml) warm water

3 cups (431g) all-purpose flour, plus more for dusting

½ tsp (2g) baking powder

1 cup (85g) cocoa powder

1 tsp (5g) Morton's kosher salt

1 cup (226g) unsalted butter, softened

1¾ cups (350g) granulated sugar

¼ cup (59ml) agave syrup

2 large eggs, room temperature

2 to 3 tbsp (30 to 45ml) whole milk, as needed

1. In a small dish, dissolve the instant coffee in the water. Stir and set aside.

2. Sift the flour, baking powder, cocoa powder, and salt into a medium bowl. Whisk to combine.

3. Add the butter and sugar to the bowl of a stand mixer fitted with the paddle attachment. Mix on medium speed until light and fluffy, about 2 minutes. Stop the mixer and scrape the bowl.

4. Add the agave syrup and dissolved instant coffee. Mix on low speed until well blended, about 1 minute.

5. Add 1 egg and mix on low speed until well blended. Stop the mixer and scrape the bowl. Add the remaining egg and mix on low speed until well blended.

6. Add the dry ingredients to the wet ingredients. Mix on low speed until everything is incorporated and the dough starts to pull away from the sides of the bowl, about 30 to 60 seconds. The dough should be soft and somewhat sticky but not so sticky that it's difficult to handle. If the dough feels too soft, add flour until it stiffens (about 2 tablespoons at a time). If the dough is very dry and crumbly, add 2 to 3 tablespoons of milk to soften.

7. Halve the dough and shape each half into a 1-inch-thick (2.5cm) rectangle. Tightly wrap in plastic wrap and refrigerate for 1 hour.

8. Roll out the dough on a floured surface to just under ¼ inch (0.65cm) and chill the sheets for 30 minutes or until firm. Cut out the desired shapes and place them on baking sheets lined with parchment paper. If the cookies are soft, refrigerate them for 15 minutes or until firm.

9. Preheat the oven to 350°F (175°C). Transfer the cookies to room temperature baking sheets lined with parchment paper.

10. Place the sheets in the oven and bake the cookies for 10 to 12 minutes or until the edges are light golden brown. Rotate the baking sheets halfway through the baking time. Remove the sheets from the oven and allow the cookies to cool completely.

GINGERBREAD COOKIES

I love how the scent of the holidays fills my whole kitchen when I bake these cookies! Enjoy them just as they are or decorate them with Vanilla Royal Icing (page 20). This yields about 36 cookies (3 inches [7.5cm] in diameter).

4 cups (575g) all-purpose flour, plus more for dusting

1 tsp (4g) baking powder

2 tsp (8g) ground ginger

1 tsp (4g) ground cinnamon

½ tsp (2g) ground cloves

½ tsp (2g) ground nutmeg

1 tsp (5g) Morton's kosher salt

1 cup (226g) unsalted butter, softened

¾ cup (150g) granulated sugar

¾ cup (160g) light brown sugar

½ cup (118ml) molasses

2 large eggs, room temperature

2 to 3 tablespoons (30 to 45ml) whole milk, as needed

1. Sift the flour, baking powder, ginger, cinnamon, cloves, nutmeg, and salt into a medium bowl. Whisk to combine.

2. Add the butter, granulated sugar, and brown sugar to the bowl of a stand mixer fitted with the paddle attachment. Mix on medium speed until light and fluffy, about 2 minutes. Stop the mixer and scrape the bowl.

3. Add the molasses and mix on low speed until well blended, about 1 minute.

4. Add 1 egg and mix on low speed until well blended. Stop the mixer and scrape the bowl. Add the remaining egg and mix on low speed until well blended.

5. Add the dry ingredients to the wet ingredients. Mix on low speed until everything is incorporated and the dough starts to pull away from the sides of the bowl, about 30 to 60 seconds. The dough should be soft and somewhat sticky but not so sticky that it's difficult to handle. If the dough feels too soft, add flour until it stiffens (about 2 tablespoons at a time). If the dough is very dry and crumbly, add 2 to 3 tablespoons of milk to soften.

6. Halve the dough and shape each half into a 1-inch-thick (2.5cm) rectangle. Tightly wrap in plastic wrap and refrigerate for 1 hour.

7. Roll out the dough on a floured surface to just under ¼ inch (0.65cm) and chill the sheets for 30 minutes or until firm. Cut out the desired shapes and place them on baking sheets lined with parchment paper. If the cookies are soft, refrigerate for 15 minutes or until firm.

8. Preheat the oven to 350°F (175°C). Transfer the cookies to room temperature baking sheets lined with parchment paper.

9. Place the sheets in the oven and bake the cookies for 10 to 12 minutes or until the edges are light golden brown. Rotate the baking sheets halfway through the baking time. Remove the sheets from the oven and allow the cookies to cool completely.

KEEPSAKE COOKIES

For those times when your cookies are too pretty to eat, you can use this recipe to save and admire your cookies for years. This is a simple cutout cookie recipe with added spices to give them a delicious aroma. This yields about 36 cookies (3 inches [7.5cm] in diameter).

4 cups (575g) all-purpose flour, plus more for dusting

1 tsp (4g) baking powder

½ tsp (2.5g) Morton's kosher salt

1 tsp (4g) ground cinnamon

½ tsp (2g) ground cloves

1 cup (226g) unsalted butter, softened

2 cups (400g) granulated sugar

1 tsp (5ml) pure vanilla extract

2 large eggs, room temperature

2 to 3 tbsp (30 to 45ml) whole milk, as needed

To save your cookies, wrap them in cellophane bags or display them in a clear box. Keep them out of direct sunlight to prevent fading. They'll last for years to come!

1. Sift the flour, baking powder, salt, cinnamon, and cloves into a medium bowl. Whisk to combine.

2. Add the butter and sugar to the bowl of a stand mixer fitted with the paddle attachment. Mix on medium speed until light and fluffy, about 2 minutes. Stop the mixer and scrape the bowl.

3. Add the vanilla extract and mix on low speed until well blended, about 1 minute.

4. Add 1 egg and mix on low speed until well blended. Stop the mixer and scrape the bowl. Add the remaining egg and mix on low speed until well blended.

5. Add the dry ingredients to the wet ingredients. Mix on low speed until everything is incorporated and the dough starts to pull away from the sides of the bowl, about 30 to 60 seconds. The dough should be soft and somewhat sticky but not so sticky that it's difficult to handle. If the dough feels too soft, add flour until it stiffens (about 2 tablespoons at a time). If the dough is very dry and crumbly, add 2 to 3 tablespoons of milk to soften. (This dough will seem drier than other recipes in this book.)

6. Halve the dough and shape each half into a 1-inch-thick (2.5cm) rectangle. Tightly wrap in plastic wrap and refrigerate for 1 hour.

7. Roll out the dough on a floured surface to just under ¼ inch (0.65cm) and chill the sheets for 30 minutes or until firm. Cut out the desired shapes and place them on baking sheets lined with parchment paper. If the cookies are soft, refrigerate for 15 minutes or until firm.

8. Preheat the oven to 350°F (175°C). Transfer the cookies to room temperature baking sheets lined with parchment paper.

9. Place the sheets in the oven and bake the cookies for 10 to 12 minutes or until the edges are light golden brown. Rotate the baking sheets halfway through the baking time. Remove the sheets from the oven and allow the cookies to cool completely.

MAPLE COOKIES

This recipe will have you craving cookies for breakfast! These maple cookies are made with maple sugar, which you can find at specialty grocery stores and online. This yields about 36 cookies (3 inches [7.5cm] in diameter).

4 cups (575g) all-purpose flour, plus more for dusting

1 tsp (4g) baking powder

½ tsp (2.5g) Morton's kosher salt

1 cup (226g) unsalted butter, softened

1 cup (200g) granulated sugar

½ cup (54g) maple sugar

½ cup (118ml) maple syrup

1 tsp (5ml) pure vanilla extract

2 large eggs, room temperature

2 to 3 tablespoons (30 to 45ml) whole milk, as needed

1. Sift the flour, baking powder, and salt into a medium bowl. Whisk to combine.

2. Add the butter, granulated sugar, and maple sugar to the bowl of a stand mixer fitted with the paddle attachment. Mix on medium speed until light and fluffy, about 2 minutes. Stop the mixer and scrape the bowl.

3. Add the maple syrup and vanilla extract. Mix on low speed until well blended, about 1 minute.

4. Add 1 egg and mix on low speed until well blended. Stop the mixer and scrape the bowl. Add the remaining egg and mix on low speed until well blended.

5. Add the dry ingredients to the wet ingredients. Mix on low speed until everything is incorporated and the dough starts to pull away from the sides of the bowl, about 30 to 60 seconds. The dough should be soft and somewhat sticky but not so sticky that it's difficult to handle. If the dough feels too soft, add flour until it stiffens (about 2 tablespoons at a time). If the dough is very dry and crumbly, add 2 to 3 tablespoons of milk to soften.

6. Halve the dough and shape each half into a 1-inch-thick (2.5cm) rectangle. Tightly wrap in plastic wrap and refrigerate for 1 hour.

7. Roll out the dough on a floured surface to just under ¼ inch (0.65cm) and chill the sheets for 30 minutes or until firm. Cut out the desired shapes and place them on baking sheets lined with parchment paper. If the cookies are soft, refrigerate them for 15 minutes or until firm.

8. Preheat the oven to 350°F (175°C). Transfer the cookies to room temperature baking sheets lined with parchment paper.

9. Place the sheets in the oven and bake the cookies for 10 to 12 minutes or until the edges are light golden brown. Rotate the baking sheets halfway through the baking time. Remove the sheets from the oven and allow the cookies to cool completely.

CONFETTI COOKIES

Break out the party hats and turn any ordinary day into a celebration with these cookies packed with rainbow sprinkles! This recipe calls for imitation vanilla, which gives these cookies a flavor reminiscent of the birthday cakes from my childhood. This yields about 36 cookies (3 inches [7.5cm] in diameter).

4 cups (575g) all-purpose flour, plus more for dusting

1 tsp (4g) baking powder

1 tsp (5g) Morton's kosher salt

1 cup (160g) rainbow sprinkles

1 cup (226g) unsalted butter, softened

1 cup (200g) granulated sugar

¾ cup (160g) light brown sugar

¼ cup (59ml) agave syrup

1 tbsp (15ml) pure vanilla extract or imitation vanilla flavor

2 large eggs, room temperature

2 to 3 tbsp (30 to 45ml) whole milk, as needed

1. Sift the flour, baking powder, and salt into a medium bowl. Add the rainbow sprinkles and whisk to combine.

2. Add the butter, granulated sugar, and brown sugar to the bowl of a stand mixer fitted with the paddle attachment. Mix on medium speed until light and fluffy, about 2 minutes. Stop the mixer and scrape the bowl.

3. Add the agave syrup and vanilla. Mix on low speed until well blended, about 1 minute.

4. Add 1 egg and mix on low speed until well blended. Stop the mixer and scrape the bowl. Add the remaining egg and mix on low speed until well blended.

5. Add the dry ingredients to the wet ingredients. Mix on low speed until everything is incorporated and the dough starts to pull away from the sides of the bowl, about 30 to 60 seconds. The dough should be soft and somewhat sticky but not so sticky that it's difficult to handle. If the dough feels too soft, add flour until it stiffens (about 2 tablespoons at a time). If the dough is very dry and crumbly, add 2 to 3 tablespoons of milk to soften.

6. Halve the dough and shape each half into a 1-inch-thick (2.5cm) rectangle. Tightly wrap in plastic wrap and refrigerate for 1 hour.

7. Roll out the dough on a floured surface to just under ¼ inch (0.65cm) and chill the sheets for 30 minutes or until firm. Cut out the desired shapes and place them on baking sheets lined with parchment paper. If the cookies are soft, refrigerate them for 15 minutes or until firm.

8. Preheat the oven to 350°F (175°C). Transfer the cookies to room temperature baking sheets lined with parchment paper.

9. Place the sheets in the oven and bake the cookies for 10 to 12 minutes or until the edges are light golden brown. Rotate the baking sheets halfway through the baking time. Remove the sheets from the oven and allow the cookies to cool completely.

MERINGUE COOKIES

Aside from decorated cookies, meringue cookies are my favorite to bake. They have a light and crispy texture, and they melt in your mouth when you bite into them. Try these sandwiched with a swirl of Whipped White Chocolate Ganache (page 41) for a dreamy treat! This yields about 42 cookies (1½ inch [3.75cm] in diameter).

3 large egg whites (½ cup), room temperature

¾ cup (300g) granulated sugar

½ tsp (2g) cream of tartar

1 tsp (5ml) pure vanilla extract

Special Equipment Needed

Thermometer

Food coloring (any colors)

Large decorating bags (16 to 18 inches [41 to 46cm])

#1M decorating tips

To create a whimsical swirl of multiple colors, scoop 3 different colors of meringue into 1 decorating bag. Or you can use a special tool like the Wilton Color Swirl coupler to easily pipe with 3 bags of meringue using 1 decorating tip.

1. Preheat the oven to 180°F (85°C).

2. Add the egg whites, sugar, and cream of tartar to the bowl of a stand mixer or a heatproof bowl. Whisk to combine.

3. Place the bowl over a pot of simmering water on the stovetop over medium-high heat. Heat the mixture to 120°F (50°C) while constantly whisking.

4. Remove the bowl from the simmering water and place it on the stand mixer fitted with the whisk attachment. (If you use a hand mixer, remove the bowl from the simmering water and place it on a dish towel or heatproof surface.)

5. Whisk on medium speed until soft peaks form, about 2 minutes.

6. Stop the mixer and add the vanilla extract. Whisk the meringue on high speed until stiff peaks form, about 2 minutes more. At this point, you can follow the instructions on pages 136–141 to make Hats & Mittens.

7. If you're making more than one color of meringue, split the meringue into separate bowls and add 1 drop of food coloring to each bowl. Add more food coloring as needed to create your desired shades.

8. Fit as many decorating bags as there are colors with a #1M decorating tip. Fill the bags with the meringue. Pipe swirls of meringue onto baking sheets lined with parchment paper.

9. Place the sheets in the oven and bake the meringue for 2 hours. Remove the sheets from the oven and allow the cookies to cool completely before removing them from the parchment paper.

PEANUT BUTTER COOKIES

I can't get enough of these peanut butter cookies! If you're a peanut butter lover like I am, I think you'll feel the same. Pair these cookies with Chocolate Royal Icing (page 37) or Chocolate Buttercream Frosting (page 40) for an extra special treat. This yields about 36 cookies (3 inches [7.5cm] in diameter).

4 cups (575g) all-purpose flour, plus more for dusting

1 tsp (4g) baking powder

1 tsp (5g) Morton's kosher salt

¾ cup (170g) unsalted butter, softened

½ cup (118ml) natural peanut butter

1 cup (200g) granulated sugar

1 cup (213g) light brown sugar

¼ cup (59ml) honey

2 tsp (10ml) pure vanilla extract

2 large eggs, room temperature

2 to 3 tbsp (30 to 45ml) whole milk, as needed

1. Sift the flour, baking powder, and salt into a medium bowl. Whisk to combine.

2. Add the butter, peanut butter, granulated sugar, and brown sugar to the bowl of a stand mixer fitted with the paddle attachment. Mix on medium speed until light and fluffy, about 2 minutes. Stop the mixer and scrape the bowl.

3. Add the honey and vanilla extract. Mix on low speed until well blended, about 1 minute.

4. Add 1 egg and mix on low speed until well blended. Stop the mixer and scrape the bowl. Add the remaining egg and mix on low speed until well blended.

5. Add the dry ingredients to the wet ingredients. Mix on low speed until everything is incorporated and the dough starts to pull away from the sides of the bowl, about 30 to 60 seconds. The dough should be soft and somewhat sticky but not so sticky that it's difficult to handle. If the dough feels too soft, add flour until it stiffens (about 2 tablespoons at a time). If the dough is very dry and crumbly, add 2 to 3 tablespoons of milk to soften.

6. Halve the dough and shape each half into a 1-inch-thick (2.5cm) rectangle. Tightly wrap in plastic wrap and refrigerate for 1 hour.

7. Roll out the dough on a floured surface to just under ¼ inch (0.65cm) and chill the sheets for 30 minutes or until firm. Cut out the desired shapes and place them on baking sheets lined with parchment paper. If the cookies are soft, refrigerate them for 15 minutes or until firm.

8. Preheat the oven to 350°F (175°C). Transfer the cookies to room temperature baking sheets lined with parchment paper.

9. Place the sheets in the oven and bake the cookies for 10 to 12 minutes or until the edges are light golden brown. Rotate the baking sheets halfway through the baking time. Remove the sheets from the oven and allow the cookies to cool completely.

STRAWBERRY COOKIES

These cookies will give you a sweet taste of summer any time of the year. This recipe calls for freeze-dried strawberries, which can be found at most grocery stores as well as online. This yields about 36 cookies (3 inches [7.5cm] in diameter).

4 cups (575g) all-purpose flour, plus more for dusting

1 tsp (4g) baking powder

1 tsp (5g) Morton's kosher salt

1 cup (226g) unsalted butter, softened

1¾ cups (350g) granulated sugar

¼ cup (59ml) agave syrup

1½ tbsp (22.5ml) pure strawberry extract

1 tsp (5ml) pure vanilla extract

1 cup (23g) freeze-dried strawberries

2 large eggs, room temperature

2 to 3 tbsp (30 to 45ml) whole milk, as needed

The freeze-dried strawberries will make the surface of the cookies a little rough, so you can flip the cookies over and decorate the back, which will be nice and smooth.

Make sure you use strawberry extract, not strawberry flavoring.

1. Sift the flour, baking powder, and salt into a medium bowl. Whisk to combine.

2. Add the butter and sugar to the bowl of a stand mixer fitted with the paddle attachment. Mix on medium speed until light and fluffy, about 2 minutes. Stop the mixer and scrape the bowl.

3. Add the agave syrup, strawberry extract, and vanilla extract. Mix on low speed until well blended, about 1 minute.

4. Add the freeze-dried strawberries and mix on low speed until well blended, about 30 seconds.

5. Add 1 egg and mix on low speed until well blended. Stop the mixer and scrape the bowl. Add the remaining egg and mix on low speed until well blended.

6. Add the dry ingredients to the wet ingredients. Mix on low speed until everything is incorporated and the dough starts to pull away from the sides of the bowl, about 30 to 60 seconds. The dough should be soft and somewhat sticky but not so sticky that it's difficult to handle. If the dough feels too soft, add flour until it stiffens (about 2 tablespoons at a time). If the dough is very dry and crumbly, add 2 to 3 tablespoons of milk to soften it.

7. Halve the dough and shape each half into a 1-inch-thick (2.5cm) rectangle. Tightly wrap in plastic wrap and refrigerate for 1 hour.

8. Roll out the dough on a floured surface to just under ¼ inch (0.65cm) and chill the sheets for 30 minutes or until firm. Cut out the desired shapes and place them on baking sheets lined with parchment paper. If the cookies are soft, refrigerate them for 15 minutes or until firm.

9. Preheat the oven to 350°F (175°C). Transfer the cookies to baking sheets lined with parchment paper.

10. Place the sheets in the oven and bake the cookies for 10 to 12 minutes or until the edges are light golden brown. Rotate the baking sheets halfway through the baking time. Remove the sheets from the oven and allow the cookies to cool completely.

CELEBRATION
COOKIES

MOTHER'S DAY

Treat your mom like royalty with these cookies fit for a queen. These tea set–inspired cookies will make a perfect addition to any Mother's Day brunch.

WHAT YOU NEED

12 baked scalloped cookies
½ cup white medium consistency royal icing
1 cup white flood consistency royal icing
2 tbsp light pink flood consistency royal icing
2 tbsp dark pink flood consistency royal icing
2 tbsp light green flood consistency royal icing
2 tbsp dark green flood consistency royal icing
Two 12-inch (30.5cm) decorating bags and couplers
4 tipless decorating bags
#1 decorating tip
#2 decorating tip
Scribe tool

NOTES

The icing measurements will make enough icing for 12 cookies. Adjust the amounts depending on how many cookies you need. See page 20 for the royal icing recipe.

For light pink icing, add a touch of Baker's Rose and a touch of Sunset Orange to 2 tablespoons of white flood consistency royal icing.

For dark pink icing, add a drop of Baker's Rose and a touch of Sunset Orange to 2 tablespoons of white flood consistency royal icing.

For light green icing, add a touch of Leaf Green and a touch of Baker's Rose to 2 tablespoons of white flood consistency royal icing.

For dark green icing, add a drop of Leaf Green and a touch of Baker's Rose to 2 tablespoons of white flood consistency royal icing.

1. Fill the tipless decorating bags with light pink, dark pink, light green, and dark green flood consistency icing.

2. Fit 1 decorating bag with a coupler and a #1 decorating tip. Fill the bag with the white medium consistency icing.

3. Fit the other decorating bag with a coupler and a #2 decorating tip. Fill the bag with the white flood consistency icing.

4. Use the bag with the #1 tip to pipe a small circle in the middle of each scallop, creating eyelets. Pipe an outline around the edge of the cookies, looping the icing between each scallop to create teardrop shapes. Pipe a larger circle in the center of the cookie, using the bottoms of the icing loops as a guide.

🕐 **Allow the icing to dry for about 30 minutes.**

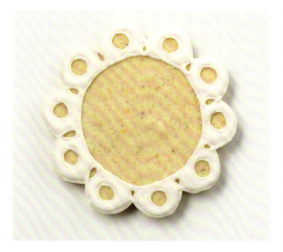

5. Use the bag with the #2 tip to fill the scallops, avoiding the small circles and teardrops. Fill the middle of the cookie.

6. Immediately use a tipless bag to pipe 4 light pink oval-shaped dots down the center of the cookies. Stagger 3 light pink oval-shaped dots on both sides of the 4 middle dots.

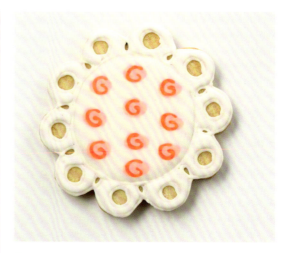

7. Use a tipless piping bag to add dark pink G-shaped swirls on top of the light pink dots.

8. Use the scribe tool to shape the 2 pink icings into roses. Start with a small spiral at the top of the dot and make wide curved motions underneath that spiral to form the petals.

9. Use a tipless bag to pipe 2 small light green dots and 2 smaller dark green dots on top at the bottom corners of each rose.

10. Starting at the edges closest to the roses, use the scribe tool to drag the light green dots down slightly to create leaves.

⏱ **Allow the icing to dry overnight.**

11. Use the bag with the #1 tip to pipe a single-bead border around the edge of the cookie and a double-bead border around the circle. (See **"How to Pipe Borders"** on page 28.)

WEDDING

Make the happy couple's day even sweeter with a gift of beautifully decorated cookies—or create a cookie for each wedding guest!

WHAT YOU NEED

- 8 baked plaque and 4 baked tiered cake cookies
- 1½ cups white flood consistency royal icing
- ¼ cup black flood consistency royal icing
- 2 tbsp gray flood consistency royal icing
- ¼ cup red stiff consistency royal icing
- 2 tbsp green stiff consistency royal icing
- 2 tbsp white stiff consistency royal icing
- 2 tbsp black medium consistency royal icing
- 2 tbsp white medium consistency royal icing
- Eight 12-inch (30.5cm) decorating bags and couplers
- #1 decorating tips
- #2 decorating tips
- #3 decorating tips
- #101 decorating tip
- #350 decorating tip
- Scribe tool
- Flower nail
- Parchment or wax paper squares
- Edible white luster dust
- Round decorator brush
- Vodka, grain alcohol, or any flavor extract
- Paint palette or small dish

NOTES

The icing measurements will make enough icing for 12 cookies. Adjust the amounts depending on how many cookies you need. See page 20 for the royal icing recipe.

For black icing, add 4 to 5 drops of Coal Black to ¼ cup of white flood consistency royal icing.

For gray icing, add a touch of black royal icing to 2 tablespoons of white flood consistency royal icing. Add more black royal icing as needed to darken the color.

For red icing, add 4 to 5 drops of Super Red to ¼ cup of white stiff consistency royal icing.

For green icing, add 2 to 3 drops of Leaf Green and a touch of Super Red to 2 tablespoons of white stiff consistency royal icing.

1. Fit a decorating bag with a coupler and a #3 decorating tip. Fill the bag with white flood consistency icing.

2. Fit a second decorating bag with a coupler and a #3 decorating tip. Fill the bag with black flood consistency icing.

3. Fit a third decorating bag with a coupler and a #1 decorating tip. Fill the bag with gray flood consistency icing.

4. Flood the 4 tiered cake cookies with the white flood consistency icing.

5. To make the gown cookies, flood 4 plaque cookies with the white flood consistency icing in the shape of a bridal gown.

6. To make the tuxedo cookies, flood an elongated upside-down triangle with the white flood consistency icing at the top of 4 plaque cookies to make the shirt.

7. Immediately fill around the shirt with black flood consistency icing to make the jacket.

8. Use the filigree template on page 197 to pipe a filigree design with gray flood consistency icing while the black icing is still wet.

9. Fit a decorating bag with a coupler and a #101 tip. Fill the bag with red stiff consistency royal icing.

10. Use a dot of icing to attach a parchment or wax paper square to the flower nail. Pipe rosebuds with the red stiff consistency icing. (See **"How to Pipe Roses"** on page 32.)

🕐 **Allow the roses and cookies to dry overnight.**

11. On a paint palette or in a small dish, combine the white luster dust and a few drops of vodka to create edible paint. Apply the luster paint to the gown cookies, the tiered cake cookies, and the white shirt of the tuxedo cookie.

12. Fit a decorating bag with a coupler and a #1 decorating tip. Fill the bag with white medium consistency icing.

13. Pipe a collar on the tuxedo cookies with the white medium consistency icing.

🕐 **Allow the icing to dry for about 20 minutes.**

14. Fit a decorating bag with a coupler and a #1 decorating tip. Fill the bag with the black flood consistency icing.

15. Pipe lapels and a bowtie on the tuxedo cookies with the black icing. Use the scribe tool to sharpen the points of the lapels and bowtie. Pipe buttons on the shirt with the black icing.

16. Fit a decorating bag with a coupler and a #2 decorating tip. Fill the bag with the white stiff consistency icing.

17. Pipe a wavy line of white stiff consistency icing on the neckline of the gown cookies. Dip the decorator brush in a little bit of water and blot it on a paper towel. Brush the icing toward the center of the cookie to create a lace texture. Work quickly so the icing doesn't dry before you have a chance to brush it. Repeat this process on the bare corners of the cookie.

Use the filigree template (page 197) to practice piping before you try it on the cookies. This design has little swirls of icing that are connected at the tail. If you look closely, you'll see that the swirls in each pair are facing away from each other. Keep this in mind while piping.

18. Pipe a filigree design (page 197) on the gown cookies and tiered cake cookies with the white medium consistency icing and a #1 decorating tip. Leave room between each tier of the cake to pipe a bead border. (See **"How to Pipe Borders"** on page 28.)

19. Pipe a bead border along each tier of the cake cookie with the white stiff consistency icing and a #2 decorating tip.

20. Fit a decorating bag with a coupler and a #350 decorating tip. Fill the bag with green stiff consistency icing.

21. Remove the roses from the parchment or wax paper squares. Attach them to the cookies with a small dot of green icing. To pipe a leaf, hold the tip so the V opening is on either side. Place the tip next to a rose and squeeze, holding the tip in place while the icing builds up. Ease up on the pressure on the bag as you pull away, creating a point on the leaf.

🕐 **Allow the icing to dry for another 2 hours before packaging the cookies.**

GIFT BOX

What's better than a box filled with treats? A box you can eat! This floral pattern was inspired by an adorable little dress my daughters wore when they were toddlers.

WHAT YOU NEED

Chilled sheets of Keepsake Cookies dough (page 50)
Cookie Box templates (page 198–199)
Flower template (page 204)
Green edible ink marker
¾ cup teal green flood consistency royal icing
½ cup dark pink flood consistency royal icing
2 tbsp dark green flood consistency royal icing
2 tbsp white flood consistency royal icing
½ cup light pink stiff consistency royal icing
2 tbsp light green stiff consistency royal icing
½ cup white stiff consistency royal icing
Three 12-inch (30.5cm) decorating bags and couplers
3 tipless decorating bags
#3 decorating tips
#5 decorating tip
Scribe tool
Small knife
Stiff decorator brush
Dish of water
Paper towel

NOTES

The icing measurements will make enough icing for 12 cookies. Adjust the amounts depending on how many cookies you need. See page 20 for the royal icing recipe.

For teal green icing, add 1 to 2 drops of Teal Green to ¾ cup of white flood consistency royal icing.

For dark pink icing, add 2 to 3 drops of Baker's Rose and a touch of Sunset Orange to ½ cup of white flood consistency royal icing.

For dark green icing, add 1 to 2 drops of Leaf Green and a touch of Baker's Rose to 2 tablespoons of white flood consistency royal icing.

For light pink icing, add 1 drop of Baker's Rose and a touch of Sunset Orange to ½ cup of white stiff consistency royal icing.

For light green icing, add 1 drop of Leaf Green and a touch of Baker's Rose to 2 tablespoons of white stiff consistency royal icing.

1. Place the Cookie Box templates on a chilled sheet of Keepsake Cookies dough and use a small knife to cut around them. Transfer the cutouts to a lined baking sheet and refrigerate or freeze for 10 to 15 minutes.

2. Preheat the oven to 350°F (175°C). Transfer the cutouts to a baking sheet lined with parchment paper. Place the sheet in the oven and bake for 11 to 12 minutes, rotating the sheet halfway through.

🕐 **Remove the sheet from the oven and allow the cookies to cool completely.**

3. Fit a 12-inch (30.5cm) decorating bag with a coupler and a #3 decorating tip. Fill the bag with teal green flood consistency icing. Fill the tipless bags with dark pink, dark green, and white flood consistency icing. Cut very small openings in the tipless bags.

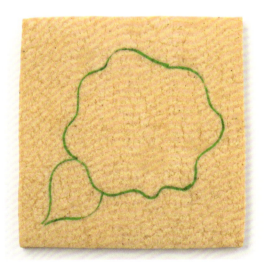

4. Use a green edible ink marker to trace the flower template on all the cutouts except for the bottom piece.

5. Flood all the cutouts (except for the bottom piece) with the teal green flood consistency icing and a #3 tip, leaving room for the flowers. Add dots with the white flood consistency icing.

6. Fill the flowers with dark pink flood consistency icing. Fill the leaf with dark green flood consistency icing. Flood 1 small round cookie with teal green flood consistency icing.

🕐 **Allow the cookies to dry overnight.**

7. Fit a decorating bag with a coupler and a #3 decorating tip. Fill the bag with light pink stiff consistency icing.

8. Outline 2 or 3 petals with light pink stiff consistency icing to create a ruffled edge.

9. Dip the stiff decorator brush into a dish of water and blot it on a dry paper towel. Brush the icing toward the center of the flower. This is known as the "brush embroidery technique."

10. Continue outlining the petals and brushing the icing inward, working with 2 or 3 petals at a time.

11. Add a smaller layer of petals over the first layer by using the brush embroidery technique. Repeat the process by using light green icing on the leaves.

12. Pipe a vein in the center of each leaf, starting at the base with heavy pressure and easing up on the pressure as you move toward the tip of the leaf. Use light green icing to pipe small dots in the center of the flower.

13. Fit a decorating bag with a coupler and a #5 decorating tip. Fill the bag with white stiff consistency icing.

14. Pipe a bead border around each iced cookie, including the small round cookie. (See **"How to Pipe Borders"** on page 28.) Attach the small round cookie to the center of the lid piece.

⏱ **Allow the icing to dry for at least 1 hour.**

15. Flip one of the long sides of the cookie box over so the iced side faces down. Pipe a wavy line of white stiff consistency icing along the short sides and along the bottom of the cookie. Flip one of the short sides over so the iced side faces down. Pipe a wavy line of icing along the bottom edge of the cookie.

16. Hold the long side of the box so it stands upright. Press the bottom edge of the cookie against the long side of the bottom piece of the box. While holding this piece in place, press the short side of the box against the bottom piece so it meets the long side of the box at the corner. Hold the pieces in place for a few seconds to make sure they stick. At this point, you should be able to let go without the pieces falling over.

17. Repeat this process with the other 2 sides of the box. Use a brush to remove any excess icing at the seams of the box.

18. Use white stiff consistency icing to pipe a bead border along the corners of the box. (See **"How to Pipe Borders"** on page 28.)

🕐 **Allow the box to dry overnight before filling with treats.**

TIPS FOR BEAUTIFUL BOXES

• You'll need 1 round cookie for this box. You can use a small round cookie cutter to make it or cut it by hand from the template provided (page 198).

• When cutting the box pieces and before you bake them, use a small knife to mark each piece to remind you which piece is which. The longer side pieces are very close in size to the top and bottom pieces, so I like to mark them with a letter indicating where each piece goes, like "L" for lid.

• If the edges of the cookies aren't straight, you can use a microplane to file them.

• When working with the brush embroidery technique, the brush should be wet enough that it easily brushes the icing but not so wet that the water pools on the cookie.

BABY ROMPER

These baby romper cookies were inspired by a floral pattern on an outfit one of my daughters wore as a baby. I created the roses by using the wet-on-wet technique.

WHAT YOU NEED

12 baked baby romper cookies
Twelve 1-inch (2.5cm) baked mini round cookies
1 cup dark blue flood consistency royal icing
3 tbsp light pink flood consistency royal icing
2 tbsp dark pink flood consistency royal icing
2 tbsp light green flood consistency royal icing
2 tbsp dark green flood consistency royal icing
¼ cup light pink stiff consistency royal icing
Two 12-inch (30.5cm) decorating bags and couplers
#3 decorating tip
#101 decorating tip
4 tipless decorating bags
Scribe tool

NOTES

The icing measurements will make enough icing for 12 cookies. Adjust the amounts depending on how many cookies you need. See page 20 for the royal icing recipe.

For dark blue icing, add 6 to 8 drops of Royal Blue and 1 to 2 drops of Coal Black to 1 cup of white flood consistency royal icing.

For light pink flood consistency icing, add a touch of Baker's Rose and a touch of Sunset Orange to 3 tablespoons of white flood consistency royal icing.

For dark pink flood consistency icing, add a drop of Baker's Rose and a touch of Sunset Orange to 2 tablespoons of white flood consistency royal icing.

For light green icing, add a touch of Leaf Green and a touch of Baker's Rose to 2 tablespoons of white flood consistency royal icing.

For dark green icing, add a drop of Leaf Green and a touch of Baker's Rose to 2 tablespoons of white flood consistency royal icing.

For light pink stiff consistency icing, add a touch of Baker's Rose and a touch of Sunset Orange to ¼ cup of white flood consistency royal icing.

1. Fit a decorating bag with a coupler and a #3 decorating tip. Fill the bag with dark blue flood consistency icing. Fill the tipless bags with the other 4 flood consistency icings. Cut very small openings in the tipless bags.

2. Flood the baby romper cookies with the dark blue flood consistency icing.

3. Immediately use a tipless bag to pipe 4 light pink oval-shaped dots down the center of the cookies. Stagger more light pink oval-shaped dots on both sides of the center dots.

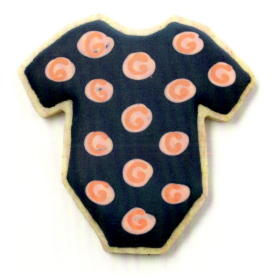

4. Use a tipless piping bag to add dark pink G-shaped swirls on top of the light pink dots.

5. Use the scribe tool to shape the 2 pink icings into roses. Start with a small spiral at the top of the dot and make wide curved motions underneath that spiral to form the petals.

6. Use a tipless bag to pipe 2 small light green dots and 2 smaller dark green dots on top at the bottom corners of each rose.

7. Starting at the edges closest to the roses, use the scribe tool to drag the light green dots down slightly to create leaves.

8. Pipe groups of 3 small light pink dots between the roses.

🕐 **Allow the icing to dry overnight.**

9. Repeat steps 2 through 7 to make a single large rose in the middle of the round cookies.

🕐 **Allow the icing to dry overnight.**

10. Fit a decorating bag with a coupler and a #3 decorating tip. Fill the bag with light pink stiff consistency icing.

11. Pipe a bead border along the neck, sleeves, and legs of the romper cookies with the pink stiff consistency icing.

TIPS FOR DECORATING WET-ON-WET ROSES

When piping the light pink dots on the dark blue icing, don't worry about shaping them perfectly. It's okay to have some dark blue icing showing through. The key is to get the dots on as quickly as possible. You'll have between 5 and 10 minutes to finish the design before the icing crusts over.

When you're shaping the roses, keep the scribe tool as close to the surface of the icing as possible. If the scribe tool goes too deep into the icing, the colors will blend too much and you'll lose the definition in the rose.

12. Switch to the #101 decorating tip and pipe 2 layers of ruffles just above the legs of the cookies, with the wide end of the tip touching the cookie and the narrow end facing toward the bottom of the cookie. Switch back to the #3 tip and pipe a bead border along the top edge of the ruffles and the outer edge of the round cookies. (See **"How to Pipe Borders"** on page 28.)

BIRTHDAY CAKE

This design was inspired by the cake my parents served at my first birthday party in the early 1980s. I used the low-tech "tissue paper method" to pipe the letters.

WHAT YOU NEED

Four 4½-inch (11.5cm) baked large round cookies

Twelve 1½-inch (4cm) baked mini round cookies

1 cup white flood consistency royal icing

1½ cups pink stiff consistency royal icing or buttercream frosting

½ cup white stiff consistency royal icing or buttercream frosting

2 tbsp green stiff consistency royal icing or buttercream frosting

2 tbsp teal green medium consistency royal icing

Five 12-inch (30.5cm) decorating bags and couplers

Teal green edible ink marker

Tissue paper

#1 decorating tip

#3 decorating tip

#16 decorating tip

#104 decorating tip

#352 decorating tip

Scribe tool

Flower nail

Parchment or wax paper squares

NOTES

The icing measurements will make enough icing for 12 cookies. Adjust the amounts depending on how many cookies you need. See page 20 for the royal icing recipe and page 39 for the buttercream frosting recipe.

For pink icing, add 2 to 3 drops of Baker's Rose to 1½ cups of white stiff consistency royal icing or buttercream frosting.

For green icing, add 1 drop of Leaf Green and a touch of Baker's Rose to 2 tablespoons of white stiff consistency royal icing or buttercream frosting.

For teal green icing, add 1 to 2 drops of Teal Green to 2 tablespoons of white medium consistency royal icing.

1. Fit a decorating bag with a coupler and a #3 decorating tip. Fill the bag with white flood consistency icing.

2. Flood the large round cookies with the white flood consistency icing. Set the cookies aside.

3. Fit a decorating bag with a coupler and a #104 decorating tip. Fill the bag with pink stiff consistency icing or pink buttercream frosting.

4. Use a dot of icing to attach a parchment or wax paper square to the flower nail. Pipe 1 large rose with 5 petals on the outer layer for each large cookie. Pipe 4 small roses with 3 petals on the outer layer for each large cookie and 1 small rose for each mini cookie. (See **"How to Pipe Roses"** on page 32.)

⏱ **Allow the roses and the cookies to dry overnight. If you're using buttercream for the roses, refrigerate them for at least 1 hour.**

5. Place a piece of tissue paper over the Happy Birthday template (page 200) and use the teal green edible ink marker to trace the lettering. Place the tissue paper on a large cookie and again use the edible ink marker to trace the lettering. The ink will bleed through the tissue paper and onto the cookie. Lift a corner of the tissue paper before removing it to make sure the ink has transferred.

6. Fit a decorating bag with a coupler and a #1 decorating tip. Fill the bag with the teal medium consistency icing. Pipe over the lettering, applying more pressure on the thicker parts of the letters. Use the scribe tool to help shape the letters as you go.

7. Fit a decorating bag with a coupler and a #16 decorating tip. Fill the bag with white stiff consistency icing or white buttercream frosting. Pipe a reverse shell border around the cookie. (See **"How to Pipe Borders"** on page 29.)

8. Fit a decorating bag with a coupler and a #352 decorating tip. Fill the bag with green stiff consistency icing or green buttercream frosting.

9. Remove the roses from the parchment or wax paper squares. Use green icing to attach the roses to the cookies and to pipe leaves around the roses. To pipe a leaf, hold the tip so the V opening is on either side. Place the tip next to the rose and squeeze, holding the tip in place while the icing builds up. Ease up on the pressure on the bag as you pull away, creating a point on the leaf.

🕐 **Allow the icing to dry for another 2 hours before packaging the cookies.**

TIPS FOR "HAPPY" BIRTHDAY COOKIES

I make the roses and the border with royal icing, but buttercream frosting would also work well. Keep in mind that buttercream doesn't dry hard like royal icing does, so carefully arrange the cookies to prevent damaging the roses.

The tissue paper you need is the same you'd use for a gift bag. Try to find one without a waxy feel, as that coating will prevent the edible ink marker from transferring onto the icing. Practice piping your lettering on a piece of parchment or wax paper before piping on the cookie.

GRADUATION

Add a little glam and a lot of sophistication to the graduation party with these marble-and-gold cookies. The graduation caps and stars are royal icing transfers you can make months ahead and store at room temperature in an airtight container. If you have leftover stars, save them for New Year's Eve celebration cookies!

WHAT YOU NEED

Twelve 2⅞-inch (7.5cm) baked plaque cookies

1¼ cups white flood consistency royal icing

¼ cup black flood consistency royal icing

¼ cup golden brown medium consistency royal icing

Three 12-inch (30.5cm) decorating bags and couplers

#1 decorating tip

#2 decorating tip

#3 decorating tip

Scribe tool

Graduation Cap & Star templates (page 204)

Wax paper

Edible black matte dust

Edible gold luster dust

Vodka, grain alcohol, or any flavor extract for painting

Paint palette or small dishes

Round decorator brush

Thin decorator brush

Glove (optional)

NOTES

The icing measurements will make enough icing for 12 cookies. Adjust the amounts depending on how many cookies you need. See page 20 for the royal icing recipe.

For black icing, add 3 to 4 drops of Coal Black to ¼ cup of white flood consistency royal icing.

For golden brown icing, add a drop of Buckeye Brown and a drop of Lemon Yellow to ¼ cup of white medium consistency royal icing.

1. Fit a decorating bag with a coupler and a #3 decorating tip. Fill the bag with white flood consistency icing.

2. On the paint palette or in a small dish, combine a small amount of edible black matte dust and a few drops of vodka.

3. Working with 1 cookie at a time, flood a plaque cookie with the white flood consistency icing.

4. Use the round decorator brush to apply branching lines of edible black paint to the icing. (Make sure to clean the round brush for later use with this project.)

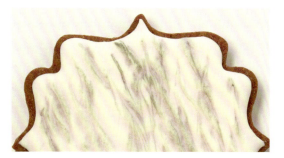

5. While the icing is still wet, drag the scribe tool through the black lines to thin them and create smaller branches. These should resemble the striations in marble. Repeat this process on the rest of the cookies.

🕐 **Allow the icing to dry overnight.**

6. Place a piece of wax paper over the Graduation Cap & Star templates.

7. Fit a decorating bag with a coupler and a #2 decorating tip. Fill the bag with black flood consistency icing.

8. Fill the bottom of each graduation cap with the black flood consistency icing and use the scribe tool to help shape the icing. Pipe black flood consistency icing for the stars. Use the scribe tool to help shape the icing and sharpen the points of the stars.

🕐 Allow the icing to dry for at least 15 minutes before filling in the tops of the graduation caps. Allow the icing to dry overnight.

9. On the paint palette or in a small dish, combine a small amount of edible gold luster dust and a few drops of vodka. Dip the round decorator brush into the edible gold paint. Use a gloved finger to flick the gold paint onto the stars. Carefully remove the royal icing transfers from the wax paper.

10. Apply a little bit of black icing to the back of the royal icing transfers to attach them to the cookies.

11. Fit a decorating bag with a coupler and a #1 decorating tip. Fill the bag with the golden brown medium consistency icing.

12. Pipe a border of your choosing around the cookies with the golden brown medium consistency icing. Pipe tassels on the graduation caps.

🕐 **Allow the icing to dry for about 1 hour.**

13. Add a few more drops of vodka to the gold luster dust if it has dried out.

14. Use the thin decorator brush to paint the golden brown border with the edible gold paint.

BACK TO SCHOOL

Make the first day back at school extra special with a few of these cookies in your kids' lunchboxes. You can use edible ink markers to write a sweet note for a fun surprise at lunchtime.

WHAT YOU NEED

Chilled sheet of cookie dough (pages 44–55)

¾ cup black flood consistency royal icing

¾ cup white flood consistency royal icing

2 tbsp pink flood consistency royal icing

2 tbsp light brown flood consistency royal icing

2 tbsp super red flood consistency royal icing

2 tbsp royal blue flood consistency royal icing

2 tbsp lemon yellow flood consistency royal icing

2 tbsp gray stiff consistency royal icing

2 tbsp golden brown stiff consistency royal icing

Red, yellow, blue, and pink edible ink markers

Cornstarch

Four 12-inch (30.5cm) decorating bags and couplers

5 tipless decorating bags

#3 decorating tips

Scribe tool

Small knife

Ruler

Thin decorator brush

Round decorator brush

NOTES

The icing measurements will make enough icing for 6 chalkboard, 6 paper, and 6 pencil cookies. Adjust the amounts depending on how many cookies you need. See page 20 for the royal icing recipe.

For black icing, add 8 to 10 drops of Coal Black to ¾ cup of white flood consistency royal icing.

For pink icing, add a touch to 1 drop of Baker's Rose and a touch of Sunset Orange to 2 tablespoons of white flood consistency royal icing.

For light brown icing, add a touch of Buckeye Brown and a touch of Lemon Yellow to 2 tablespoons of white flood consistency royal icing.

For super red icing, add 2 to 3 drops of Super Red to 2 tablespoons of white flood consistency royal icing.

For royal blue icing, add 2 to 3 drops of Royal Blue to 2 tablespoons of white flood consistency royal icing.

For lemon yellow icing, add 2 to 3 drops of Lemon Yellow to 2 tablespoons of white flood consistency royal icing.

For gray icing, add a touch of black icing to 2 tablespoons of white stiff consistency royal icing.

For golden brown icing, add a drop of Buckeye Brown and a drop of Lemon Yellow to 2 tablespoons of white stiff consistency royal icing.

1. Preheat the oven to 350°F (175°C).

2. Use the ruler and small knife to measure and cut 3½- x 2½-inch (9 x 6cm) rectangles for the chalkboard and paper cookies.

3. Use the ruler and small knife to measure and cut 3½- x ¾-inch (9 x 2cm) strips for the pencils. Trim 1 end of each cutout to make a point. Place all the cutouts on 2 baking sheets.

4. Place the sheets in the oven and bake the cookies for 10 to 12 minutes. Remove the sheets from the oven.

🔴 **Allow the cookies to cool completely.**

5. Fill the tipless decorating bags with pink, light brown, super red, royal blue, and lemon yellow flood consistency icing.

TO MAKE THE PENCIL COOKIES

1. Working with 2 cookies at a time, flood 2 pencil cookies with royal blue icing, leaving the ends blank.

2. Immediately fill the pointed ends of the pencils with light brown icing, leaving the tips blank. Fill the tips with royal blue icing. Drag the scribe tool through the blue icing toward the tip to create points in the light brown icing.

3. Fill the erasers with pink icing. Repeat these steps with the remaining pencil cookies, using super red and lemon yellow icing.

⏱ **Allow the icing to dry overnight.**

4. Fit a decorating bag with a coupler and a #3 decorating tip. Fill the bag with gray stiff consistency icing.

5. Draw vertical lines on the pencils using edible ink markers in the same color as the icing. Pipe horizontal lines with gray icing where the eraser meets the pencil.

⏱ **Allow the icing to dry for at least 1 hour before packaging the cookies.**

TO MAKE THE CHALKBOARD COOKIES

1. Fit a decorating bag with a coupler and a #3 decorating tip. Fill the bag with black flood consistency icing.

2. Flood 6 rectangle cookies with black icing.

🕐 **Allow the icing to dry overnight.**

3. Fit a decorating bag with a coupler and a #3 decorating tip. Fill the bag with golden brown stiff consistency icing.

4. Outline the cookies with golden brown icing.

5. Use the scribe tool to write "back to school" or any message you'd like in the icing.

6. Pipe over the lettering with the super red, lemon yellow, and royal blue icing in the tipless decorating bags. Use the thin decorating brush to remove some of the icing from the lettering.

🕐 **Allow the icing to dry for about 15 minutes.**

7. To create a chalky effect, use the round decorating brush and the cornstarch to dust the letters and chalkboard.

TO MAKE THE PAPER COOKIES

1. Fit a decorating bag with a coupler and a #3 decorating tip. Fill the bag with white flood consistency icing.

2. Turn 6 rectangle cookies so the short edges are at the top and bottom of your work surface. Flood the cookies with white icing. Immediately pipe 3 dots with black icing (from the chalkboard) along the left-hand side of the cookies.

🔴 **Allow the icing to dry overnight.**

3. Use a piece of paper to draw a straight line with the pink edible ink marker on the right-hand side of the black dots.

4. Draw horizontal lines with the blue edible ink marker on the cookies, spacing the lines ⅜ inch (1cm) apart.

SEASONAL COOKIES

VALENTINE'S DAY

Express your true feelings to your Valentine with these brightly colored leopard print cookies. This design uses the wet-on-wet technique, which means you'll only need flood consistency icing to decorate this set.

WHAT YOU NEED

12 baked heart cookies
1 cup white flood consistency royal icing
1 cup deep pink flood consistency royal icing
3 tbsp sky blue flood consistency royal icing
¼ cup black flood consistency royal icing
Scribe tool
Three 12-inch (30.5cm) decorating bags and couplers
1 tipless decorating bag
#1 decorating tip
#3 decorating tips
Small spatula

NOTES

The icing measurements will make enough icing for 12 cookies. Adjust the amounts depending on how many cookies you need. See page 20 for the royal icing recipe.

For deep pink icing, add 1 drop of Deep Pink to 1 cup of white flood consistency royal icing.

For sky blue icing, add 1 drop of Sky Blue to 3 tablespoons of white flood consistency royal icing.

For black icing, add 6 drops of Coal Black to ¼ cup of white flood consistency royal icing.

1. Fit 2 decorating bags with a coupler and a #3 decorating tip. Fill 1 bag with white icing and the other bag with deep pink icing.

2. Fit a decorating bag with a coupler and a #1 decorating tip. Fill the bag with black icing. Fill the tipless decorating bag with sky blue icing.

3. Pipe alternating vertical stripes about 1 inch (2.5cm) thick in pink and white icing. Use a small spatula to blend the colors where they meet.

4. Pipe small spots with sky blue icing all over each cookie. Outline the spots with black icing. Don't outline them all the way around—leave some space to resemble a leopard's spots.

🕐 **Allow the icing to dry for about 1 hour.**

5. Pipe a dotted border around the cookies with sky blue icing. (See **"How to Pipe Borders"** on page 28.)

🕐 **Allow the icing to dry overnight.**

TULIP BOUQUET

An edible bouquet is the perfect centerpiece to display at Sunday brunch—but this one is made from cookies! Feel free to use any colors you like to create your own unique tulips. You can also use this technique to turn nearly any cookie into a cookie pop!

WHAT YOU NEED

12 baked tulip cookies

Chilled sheet of cookie dough (pages 44–55)

1¼ cups lemon yellow flood consistency royal icing

2 tbsp green flood consistency royal icing

½ cup deep pink stiff consistency royal icing

Three 12-inch (30.5cm) decorating bags and couplers

#1 decorating tip

#2 decorating tip

#3 decorating tip

12 oven-safe cookie sticks

Scribe tool

Small knife

Stiff decorator brush

Dish of water

Dry cloth or paper towel

NOTES

The icing measurements will make enough icing for 12 cookies. Adjust the amounts depending on how many cookies you need. See page 20 for the royal icing recipe.

For lemon yellow icing, add 2 to 3 drops of Lemon Yellow to 1¼ cups of white flood consistency icing.

For green icing, add 1 drop of Leaf Green and a touch of Deep Pink to 2 tablespoons of white flood consistency icing.

For deep pink icing, add 2 to 3 drops of Deep Pink to ½ cup of white stiff consistency icing.

1. Preheat the oven to 350°F (175°C).

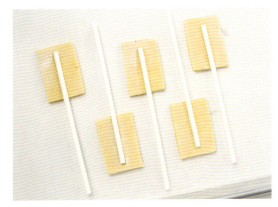

2. Cut the cookie dough into twelve 2- x 1½-inch (5 x 4cm) rectangles. Brush the dough with a little water and press a cookie stick into each rectangle to resemble a lollipop. Place the rectangles on a baking sheet, with the sticks facing up.

3. Place the sheet in the oven and bake the cookies for 9 to 10 minutes. Remove the sheet from the oven.

❷ Allow the cookies to cool completely.

4. Fit a decorating bag with a coupler and a #3 decorating tip. Fill the bag with lemon yellow icing. Fit another decorating bag with a coupler and a #1 decorating tip. Fill with green icing.

5. Flood the tulip cookies with the lemon yellow icing. Fill the stems with the green icing.

❷ Allow the cookies to dry overnight.

6. Fit a decorating bag with a coupler and a #2 decorating tip. Fill the bag with deep pink icing.

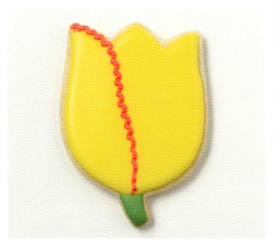

7. Pipe a wavy line of deep pink icing from the top of the left petal to the stem to create petal borders. (You can use the scribe tool to mark the borders before icing.)

8. Dip the stiff decorator brush into the dish of water and blot it on a dry cloth or paper towel. Brush the icing toward the bottom corner of the petal. If the icing is drying before you have a chance to brush it, pipe shorter lines.

9. Repeat steps 7 and 8 to create a second petal on the right side. Pipe a wavy line of deep pink icing across the middle petal and repeat step 8 to create the middle petal, which should look like it's overlapped by the 2 outer petals.

10. Apply a little deep pink icing on top of the cookie sticks. Press a rectangle cookie to the back of each tulip cookie.

🕐 **Allow the cookies to dry for about 2 hours.**

11. Fill a large Mason jar or large vase with granulated sugar. Arrange the cookie pops in the jar and vase, using the sugar to help keep them in place.

MARBLED EGGS

Instead of dyeing real eggs next Easter, try dipping some egg cookies! They're just as much fun (if not more!), and in my humble opinion, they're much more delicious. Because the cookies turn out different from each other, it's like getting a little surprise each time.

WHAT YOU NEED

12 baked egg cookies
2 cups white flood consistency royal icing
Deep Pink food coloring
Sky Blue food coloring
Violet food coloring
Paint palette or small dishes
Shallow dish or plate
Round decorator brush

NOTES

The icing measurements will make enough icing for 12 cookies. Adjust the amounts depending on how many cookies you need. See page 20 for the royal icing recipe.

1. On a paint palette or on small dishes, place 1 or 2 drops of each color of food coloring. Add a few drops of water to each color to dilute.

2. Place a small amount of white flood consistency icing on a shallow dish or plate. Dip the round decorator brush into 1 color at a time and dot the surface of the icing with the brush. Clean the brush between each color.

3. Use the brush to swirl the colors on the plate.

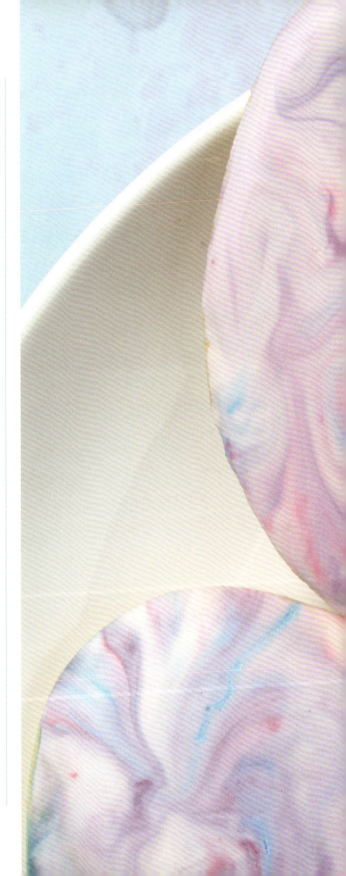

4. Dip a cookie into the icing. Twist the cookie back and forth a bit to make sure the whole front of the cookie is covered. Remove the cookie from the icing and dip it again, moving the cookie to a different spot on the plate. Keep dipping the cookie while checking it periodically to make sure the colors are marbling. If there isn't enough color, add more food coloring, repeat the dotting method with the round brush, and dip the cookie again.

5. You'll need to refill the plate with more white flood consistency icing and food coloring between each cookie or between every 2 cookies. Clean up the edges of the cookies with a finger or the round brush.

⏱ **Place the cookies on a flat surface to allow the icing to dry overnight before packaging or displaying on a platter.**

LANTERNS & STARS

Light up the night with these glowing lanterns and shining star cookies! These are fabulous additions to any dessert table, including at an Eid celebration or a summer evening party.

WHAT YOU NEED

12 baked plaque cookies and 12 baked star cookies

3 tbsp black flood consistency royal icing

¾ cup dark purple flood consistency royal icing

¾ cup dark blue flood consistency royal icing

½ cup deep pink flood consistency royal icing

½ cup white flood consistency royal icing

¼ cup white medium consistency royal icing

Six 12-inch (30.5cm) decorating bags and couplers

#1 decorating tip

#2 decorating tips

Scribe tool

Tapered spatula

Lantern template (page 203)

Edible white matte dust

Round decorator brush

NOTES

The icing measurements will make enough icing for 12 lantern cookies and 12 star cookies. Adjust the amounts depending on how many cookies you need. See page 20 for the royal icing recipe.

For black icing, add 4 drops of Coal Black to 3 tablespoons of white flood consistency royal icing.

For dark purple icing, add 2 drops of Violet and a touch of Deep Pink to ¾ cup of white flood consistency royal icing.

For dark blue icing, add 2 drops of Royal Blue and a touch of Coal Black to ¾ cup of white flood consistency royal icing.

For deep pink icing, add 1 drop of Deep Pink to ½ cup of white flood consistency royal icing.

1. Fit 4 decorating bags with a coupler and a #2 decorating tip. Fill the bags with black, dark blue, dark purple, and deep pink flood consistency icing. Fit another decorating bag with a coupler and a #1 decorating tip. Fill that bag with white flood consistency icing.

2. Working with 1 cookie at a time, flood the top half of a plaque cookie with dark blue icing. Flood the bottom half with dark purple icing.

3. Use a tapered spatula to blend the colors in the middle.

🕐 **Allow the cookies to dry overnight. Begin decorating the star cookies while the lantern cookies dry.**

4. Working with 1 cookie at a time, outline a star cookie with black icing. Make a small circle in the middle of the cookie with the white flood consistency icing. With the deep pink, dark purple, and dark blue icing, make star-shaped rings to fill the rest of the cookie, leaving the black outline.

5. Move the tapered spatula in a swirling motion to blend the colors.

6. While the icing is still wet, pipe 2 large dots near the center of the cookie with white flood consistency icing.

7. Drag the scribe tool through each dot to create points for the stars, wiping the tool on a damp cloth or paper towel between each swipe.

8. Pipe several small dots around the stars with white flood consistency icing.

🕐 **Allow the icing to dry overnight.**

9. Fit a decorating bag with a coupler and a #1 decorating tip. Fill the bag with white medium consistency icing.

10. Use the scribe tool to trace the lantern template on the dried plaque cookies. Pipe the lanterns with white medium consistency icing.

🕐 **Allow the icing to dry for about 2 hours.**

11. Dust the cookies with edible white matte dust to create a glowing effect around the lanterns. Apply the dust so it's concentrated in the center and faded toward the edges.

12. Pipe a border around the cookies with white medium consistency icing.

SUMMER BBQ

Treat the king or queen of the grill in your life to a sweet surprise with these hamburger cookies—complete with onions, tomatoes, and pickles!

WHAT YOU NEED

Chilled sheet of cookie dough (pages 44–55)
2½- x 3½-inch (6.5 x 7.5cm) rectangle cookie cutter
Twelve 2½-inch (6.5cm) baked round cookies
Six 1½-inch (4cm) baked round cookies
⅓ cup light brown flood consistency royal icing
2 tbsp lemon yellow flood consistency royal icing
¼ cup white flood consistency royal icing
3 tbsp purple flood consistency royal icing
3 tbsp super red flood consistency royal icing
¼ cup orange flood consistency royal icing
3 tbsp light green flood consistency royal icing
3 tbsp dark green flood consistency royal icing
2 tbsp dark brown medium consistency royal icing
Eight 12-inch (30.5cm) decorating bags and couplers
#1 decorating tips
#2 decorating tip
Scribe tool
Small knife
Round decorator brush
Brown edible ink marker

NOTES

The icing measurements will make enough icing for 12 hamburger, 6 onion, 6 tomato, and 6 pickle cookies. Adjust the amounts depending on how many cookies you need. See page 20 for the royal icing recipe.

For dark brown icing, add 2 drops of Buckeye Brown and a touch of Coal Black to 2 tablespoons of white medium consistency royal icing.

For light brown icing, add ½ teaspoon of dark brown icing to ⅓ cup of white flood consistency icing. Add more dark brown icing to the light brown icing as needed to adjust the color.

For lemon yellow icing, add 1 drop of Lemon Yellow to 2 tbsp of white flood consistency icing.

For purple icing, add 1 drop of Violet food coloring plus a touch of Deep Pink food coloring to 3 tablespoons of white flood consistency royal icing.

For super red icing, add 2 drops of Super Red to 3 tablespoons of white flood consistency royal icing.

For orange icing, add a touch of Super Red and 1 drop of Lemon Yellow to ¼ cup of white flood consistency royal icing.

For dark green icing, add 2 drops of Leaf Green plus a touch of Super Red to 3 tablespoons of white flood consistency royal icing.

For light green icing, add ½ teaspoon of dark green icing to 3 tablespoons of white flood consistency icing. Add more dark green icing to the light green icing as needed to adjust the color.

1. Preheat the oven to 350°F (175°C). Cut the cookie dough into 12 rectangles. Use a small knife to trim the corners so they're rounded. Place the cutouts on a baking sheet.

2. Place the sheet in the oven and bake the cookies for 10 to 12 minutes. Remove the sheet from the oven and allow the cookies to cool completely before icing.

3. Use the edible ink marker to outline the buns and the hamburger patty on the rectangle cookies. Use the round decorator brush to apply dark brown icing in the hamburger patty outline. Stipple the brush to create texture.

⏱ **Allow the icing to dry for about 20 minutes.**

4. Fit a decorating bag with a coupler and a #1 decorating tip. Fill the bag with lemon yellow icing.

5. Pipe a triangle of lemon yellow icing on each hamburger for the cheese.

⏱ **Allow the icing to dry for about 15 minutes.**

6. Fit a decorating bag with a coupler and a #1 decorating tip. Fill the bag with super red icing.

7. Pipe an elongated rectangle of super red icing above each hamburger for the tomato slice.

⏱ **Allow the icing to dry for about 20 minutes.**

8. Fit a decorating bag with a coupler and a #1 decorating tip. Fill the bag with light green icing.

9. Pipe a thick, wavy line of light green icing above each tomato for the lettuce.

⏱ **Allow the icing to dry for about 20 minutes.**

10. Fit a decorating bag with a coupler and a #2 decorating tip. Fill the bag with light brown icing.

11. Flood the top and bottom buns with the light brown icing, ensuring you cover the outlines you marked earlier.

12. Fit a decorating bag with a coupler and a #1 decorating tip. Fill the bag with purple icing. Fit another decorating bag with a coupler and a #1 decorating tip. Fill the bag with white icing.

13. On 6 of the 2½-inch (6.5cm) round cookies, pipe rings of purple icing to make the onions.

14. Immediately fill the rest of the cookie with white icing.

15. Use the scribe tool to blend the white and purple icings where they meet. Use the scribe tool to also draw a small, thin circle of purple icing in the center of each onion.

16. Fit a decorating bag with a coupler and the #1 decorating tip. Fill the bag with orange icing. You'll also need the super red icing and a #1 decorating tip from the hamburger cookies.

17. On 6 of the 2½ round (6.5cm) cookies, pipe a thick outline with super red icing. Pipe 3 rounded triangles around the center of each cookie.

18. Immediately fill the rest of the cookies with orange icing.

19. While the red icing is still wet, pipe seeds in the red triangles with orange icing.

20. Fit a decorating bag with a coupler and a #1 decorating tip. Fill the bag with dark green icing. You'll also need the light green icing and the #1 decorating tip from the hamburger cookies.

21. On the 1½-inch (4cm) round cookies, pipe a wavy outline with dark green icing. Pipe 3 rounded triangles around the center of each cookie.

22. Immediately fill the rest of the cookies with light green icing.

23. While the icing is still wet, pipe seeds in the dark green triangles with light green icing.

24. On a large platter, arrange the hamburger, onion, tomato, and pickle cookies.

GOTH PUMPKINS

Adorned with silver luster dust and black royal icing roses, these pumpkin cookies are ready for one very elegant Halloween party.

WHAT YOU NEED

12 baked pumpkin cookies
¾ cup white flood consistency royal icing
¾ cup black flood consistency royal icing
1 cup black stiff consistency royal icing
Scribe tool
Three 12-inch (30.5cm) decorating bags and couplers
#2 decorating tips
#3 decorating tip
#101 decorating tip
#350 decorating tip
Parchment or wax paper squares
Flower nail
Thin decorator brush
Round decorator brush
Edible silver luster dust
Edible white luster dust
Vodka, grain alcohol, or any flavor extract
Paint palette or small dish

NOTES

The icing measurements will make enough icing for 12 cookies. Adjust the amounts depending on how many cookies you need. See page 20 for the royal icing recipe.

For black icing, add 10 drops of Coal Black to 1¾ cups of white stiff consistency icing. Separate ¾ cup of black stiff consistency icing and thin it to flood consistency by following the instructions on page 19.

1. Fit a decorating bag with a coupler and a #2 decorating tip. Fill the bag with white flood consistency icing. Fit another bag with a coupler and a #2 decorating tip. Fill the bag with black flood consistency icing.

2. Flood the middle and 2 outer sections of the pumpkin cookies with black flood consistency icing. Leave a V indentation in the middle section for the stem.

🕑 **Allow the icing to dry for about 30 minutes.**

3. Flood the remaining 2 sections with the white flood consistency icing.

🕑 **Allow the icing to dry for about 1 hour.**

4. Fit a decorating bag with a coupler and a #3 decorating tip. Fill the bag with black stiff consistency icing.

5. Pipe stems on the cookies with black stiff consistency icing. Create texture on the stems by moving the piping tip up and down along the length of the stem as you pipe. Use the black stiff consistency icing to pipe curly vines on the cookies in any pattern you prefer.

6. Switch the tip on the black stiff consistency icing to a #101 decorating tip. Use a dot of icing to attach a parchment or wax paper square to the flower nail. Pipe roses on the parchment with black stiff consistency icing. (See **"How to Pipe Roses"** on page 32.) You'll need a 5-petal rose and two 3-petal rosebuds for each cookie.

◷ Allow the roses and the cookies to dry overnight. Save the leftover black stiff consistency icing for the following day. (See page 20 for how to store leftover icing for later use.)

7. Place a little bit of silver luster dust on a paint palette or in a small dish. Add a few drops of vodka to create an edible paint.

8. Use the thin decorator brush to apply the edible silver paint to the stems and vines on the pumpkin cookies. Use the round decorator brush to dust the roses with white luster dust.

9. Fit a decorating bag with a coupler and a #350 decorating tip. Fill the decorating bag with black stiff consistency icing.

10. Attach the roses to the cookies with a little bit of black stiff consistency icing. Pipe 1 or 2 leaves next to each rose. (See page 61 for instructions on how to pipe leaves.)

Worried about color bleed when applying black and whites icing right next to each other? Read my tips on how to prevent color bleed on page 33.

HALLOWEEN

Bright orange and yellow against dark purple create an eerie glowing effect on these jack-o'-lantern cookies. Get creative with the faces to make your own unique Halloween treats!

WHAT YOU NEED

12 baked pumpkin cookies

¼ cup white medium consistency royal icing

1¼ cups dark purple flood consistency royal icing

¼ cup dark purple stiff consistency royal icing

Small spatula

Scribe tool

Two 12-inch (30.5cm) decorating bags and couplers

#3 decorating tip

Round decorator brush

Yellow edible ink marker

Orange edible ink marker

Vodka, grain alcohol, or another flavor extract

Small dish

Paper towel or dry cloth

NOTES

The icing measurements will make enough icing for 12 cookies. Adjust the amounts depending on how many cookies you need. See page 20 for the royal icing recipe.

For dark purple icing, add 5 to 6 drops of Violet and 2 to 3 drops of Royal Blue to 1½ cups of white stiff consistency icing. Separate ¼ cup of purple stiff consistency icing. Thin the remaining 1¼ cups of purple stiff icing to flood consistency by following the instructions on page 19.

When blending the colors with the brush, make sure to keep the yellow areas bright to enhance the glowing effect. If you accidentally get some orange in the middle, clean off the brush and use it to remove some of the orange color.

1. Use a small spatula to spread a thin layer of white medium consistency icing on each pumpkin cookie.

🕐 **Allow the icing to dry for 30 to 60 minutes.**

2. Use the orange edible ink marker to draw a thick outline to create the mouth and eyes. Use the same marker to draw 5 vertical sections on the pumpkin, avoiding the eyes and mouth. These represent the pumpkin's ribs. Use the yellow edible ink marker to color in the outlines.

3. Add a little vodka to a small dish. Dip the round decorator brush into the vodka, blotting the excess on a paper towel or a dry cloth. Use the brush to blend the orange and yellow for the mouth and eyes.

5. Flood the remaining 2 sections with dark purple flood consistency icing.

🕐 **Allow the icing to dry for 1 hour more.**

4. Fit a decorating bag with a coupler and a #3 decorating tip. Fill the bag with dark purple flood consistency icing. Use the bag to flood the middle and outer sections of the pumpkin with the icing.

🕐 **Allow the icing to dry for at least 1 hour.**

6. Fit another decorating bag with a coupler and a #3 decorating tip. Fill the bag with dark purple stiff consistency icing. Use the bag to pipe a stem with the icing. Create texture on the stem by moving the tip up and down along the length of the stem as you pipe.

FALL BOUQUET

Living in New York, I've experienced some truly picturesque fall days, complete with gorgeous foliage, bright blue skies, and a chill in the air. No matter where you are in the world, this edible bouquet of colorful leaves and golden yellow chrysanthemums in a textured filigree vase will capture the beauty of the season for you to share with loved ones.

WHAT YOU NEED

Chilled sheet of cookie dough (pages 44–55)
Vase template (page 201)
Filigree template (page 197)
Twelve 3-inch (7.5cm) baked leaf cookies
¼ cup dark brown flood consistency royal icing
¼ cup green flood consistency royal icing
¼ cup sunset orange flood consistency royal icing
¼ cup yellow flood consistency royal icing
¼ cup super red flood consistency royal icing
¼ cup blue flood consistency royal icing
¼ cup white stiff consistency royal icing, thinned slightly with water
½ cup golden yellow stiff consistency royal icing or buttercream
¼ cup green stiff consistency royal icing or buttercream
Scribe tool
Small knife
Wire cooling rack
Three 12-inch (30.5cm) decorating bags and couplers
6 tipless decorating bags
#5 decorating tip
#59s decorating tip
#352 decorating tip
Round decorator brush
Parchment or wax paper squares
Flower nail

NOTES

The icing measurements will make enough icing for 1 large vase cookie, 12 leaf cookies, and 6 chrysanthemum cookies. Adjust the amounts depending on how many cookies you need. See page 20 for the royal icing recipe.

For dark brown icing, add 2 to 3 drops of Buckeye Brown to ¼ cup of white flood consistency icing.

For green flood consistency icing, add 2 to 3 drops of Leaf Green to ¼ cup of white flood consistency icing.

For sunset orange icing, add 1 to 2 drops of Sunset Orange to ¼ cup of white flood consistency icing.

For yellow icing, add 1 to 2 drops of Lemon Yellow and a touch of Sunset Orange to ¼ cup of white flood consistency icing.

For super red icing, add 2 to 3 drops of Super Red to ¼ cup of white flood consistency icing.

For blue icing, add ½ to 1 drop of Royal Blue and a touch of Coal Black to ¼ cup of white flood consistency icing.

For golden yellow icing, add 2 to 3 drops of Lemon Yellow plus ½ drop of Sunset Orange to ½ cup of white stiff consistency icing.

For green stiff consistency icing, add 1 drop of Leaf Green plus a touch of Super Red to ¼ cup of white stiff consistency icing.

1. Preheat the oven to 350°F (175°C).

2. Use the small knife and the vase template to cut a vase cookie from the chilled cookie dough. Place the cutout on a baking sheet.

3. Place the sheet in the oven and bake the cookie for 12 to 14 minutes. Remove the sheet from the oven.

⏱ **Allow the cookie to cool completely.**

4. Fit a 12-inch (30.5cm) decorating bag with a coupler and a #5 decorating tip. Fill the bag with white icing.

Use the filigree template (page 197) to practice piping before decorating the vase cookie. Or use the tissue paper method shown on page 79 to transfer the filigree design onto the cookie and pipe over it.

5. Pipe a filigree design with white icing on the vase cookie.

🕐 **Allow the icing to dry for about 1 hour.**

6. Place a wire cooling rack over a baking sheet lined with parchment paper. Place the vase cookie on the rack.

7. Fill a tipless decorating bag with blue icing. Cut a small hole in the bag and cover the entire cookie with the blue icing, allowing it to drip over the edges of the cookie. Hold the cookie upright and shake it a bit to remove excess icing. Use the round decorator brush to remove excess icing from the crevices and to clean up the edges. This might take several minutes. Place the cookie on a clean surface.

🕐 **Allow the icing to dry overnight.**

8. Fill the remaining tipless decorating bags with super red, sunset orange, yellow, green, and dark brown flood consistency icing.

11. Fit a 12-inch (30.5cm) decorating bag with a coupler and a #59s decorating tip. Fill the bag with golden yellow stiff consistency royal icing or buttercream.

9. Cut a small hole in each tipless decorating bag. Working with 1 leaf at a time, apply several splotches of each color to the cookie.

12. Use a dot of icing to attach a parchment or wax paper square to the flower nail. Hold the tip so the curve is up, like a smile. The narrow end of the tip should face out and the wide end should touch the parchment paper. While turning the flower nail, use a wavy motion to pipe a circle of icing. This will be the first layer of petals.

10. Use the scribe tool to swirl the icings together to create a marbled design. Create the illusion of veins by dragging the scribe tool from each point of the leaf to the center of the cookie.

🕐 **Allow the cookies to dry overnight.**

13. Pipe another smaller layer of petals on top using the same motion.

14. Continue building smaller and smaller layers until you reach the center of the flower.

15. Fit a 12-inch (30.5cm) decorating bag with a coupler and a #352 decorating tip. Fill the bag with green stiff consistency royal icing or buttercream.

16. Hold the tip so the V shapes are on the sides. Place the tip as close to the flower as possible and squeeze to let the icing build up. Move the tip forward and backward a few times while squeezing the bag to create waves in the leaf. Release the pressure and pull the tip away from the leaf. Repeat this flower-making process to create 2 more flowers with leaves.

🕐 **Allow the flowers and their leaves to dry overnight. If you're using buttercream, refrigerate until firm.**

17. Arrange the vase and leaf cookies on a platter. Remove the flowers and their leaves from the parchment paper squares and place them among the leaves.

CHRISTMAS TREES

These are the coziest-looking cookies I've ever decorated! I'm not sure if I should eat them or snuggle up on the couch with them. Filling the squares to create a plaid pattern takes time and patience, but the result is worth it!

WHAT YOU NEED

36 baked gingerbread cookies (page 49) cut into Christmas trees
¼ cup brown flood consistency royal icing
¼ cup red flood consistency royal icing
½ cup black flood consistency royal icing
¼ cup light green flood consistency royal icing
¼ cup dark green flood consistency royal icing
1 cup white flood consistency royal icing
½ cup light beige medium consistency royal icing
Scribe tool
Eight 12-inch (30.5cm) decorating bags and couplers
#1 decorating tips
#3 decorating tip
Black edible ink marker
White sanding sugar or granulated sugar
Edible gold luster dust
Vodka, grain alcohol, or any flavor extract
Round decorator brush
Paint palette or small dish
Shallow dish
Ruler

NOTES

The icing measurements will make enough icing for 12 red cookies, 12 green cookies, and 12 white cookies. Adjust the amounts depending on how many cookies you need. See page 20 for the royal icing recipe.

For brown icing, add 2 to 3 drops of Buckeye Brown to ¼ cup of white flood consistency icing.

For red icing, add 2 to 3 drops of Super Red and a touch of Coal Black to ¼ cup of white flood consistency icing.

For black icing, add 5 to 6 drops of Coal Black to ½ cup of white flood consistency icing.

For light green icing, add 1 to 2 drops of Leaf Green to ¼ cup of white flood consistency icing.

For dark green icing, add 2 to 3 drops of Forest Green to ¼ cup of white flood consistency icing.

For light beige icing, add a touch of Buckeye Brown to ½ cup of white medium consistency icing.

1. To make the red plaid cookies, use the ruler and the black edible ink marker to draw a ⅜-inch (1cm) grid on 12 gingerbread cookies.

2. Fit 3 decorating bags with a coupler and a #1 decorating tip. Fill the bags with red, brown, and black icing.

3. Fill every other square with brown icing to create a checkerboard pattern.

4. Fill the empty squares in every other row with black icing.

5. Fill the remaining squares with red icing.

🕐 **Allow the icing to dry for at least 2 hours or overnight.**

6. Fit a decorating bag with a coupler and a #3 decorating tip. Fill the bag with light beige icing.

7. Place the sugar in the shallow dish. Pipe an outline with light beige icing around the cookies. Dip the cookies into the sugar.

8. To make the green plaid cookies, repeat steps 1 through 7, but use green and dark green icing (as well as black icing) for the squares. Draw a ⅜-inch (1cm) grid on each cookie using a ruler and the black edible ink marker.

9. To make the white plaid cookies, fit a decorating bag with a coupler and a #3 decorating tip. Fill the bag with white icing.

11. While the base layer is still wet, pipe horizontal stripes with black icing, spacing them about 1 inch (2.5cm) apart.

12. Pipe 1 stripe above and below each horizontal stripe to make groups of 3 stripes.

🕐 **Allow the icing to dry overnight.**

10. Working with 1 cookie at a time, flood the cookie with white icing. Immediately pipe 3 pairs of vertical stripes with black icing and a #1 decorating tip, spacing each pair about ¾ inch (2cm) apart.

13. Pipe an outline around the cookies with light beige icing and a #3 decorating tip. Allow the icing to dry for about 1 hour.

14. Place a small amount of gold luster dust on a paint palette or in small dish. Add a few drops of vodka. Use the round decorating brush to apply the gold luster paint to the light beige outline.

HATS & MITTENS

These cable-knit hats and mittens are almost too cute to eat! Once you try one, you might not be able to resist eating the whole batch. Light and crispy meringue cookies are one of my favorite treats!

WHAT YOU NEED

Meringue Cookies recipe (page 53)

Hat & Mitten template (page 205)

Teal green gel food coloring

Deep pink gel food coloring

Two 12-inch (30.5cm) decorating bags and couplers

#3 decorating tip

#8 decorating tips

#16 decorating tip

Tapered spatula

Round decorator brush

Small dish

Shallow dish

White sanding sugar or granulated sugar

NOTES

The measurements will make enough meringue for 20 hat cookies and 20 mitten cookies. Make an extra cookie of either type to use for "glue." Adjust the amounts depending on how many cookies you need.

1. Preheat the oven to 180°F (85°C).

2. Trace the hat and mitten template on a piece of parchment paper. You can fit 12 of each shape on a half-sheet size of parchment. Place the template on a baking sheet and place another piece of parchment paper on top.

3. Split the meringue recipe into 2 bowls. Add 2 to 3 drops of teal green food coloring to 1 bowl and 2 to 3 drops of deep pink food coloring to the other bowl.

4. Fit 2 decorating bags with a coupler and a #8 decorating tip. Fill the bags with the meringue.

5. Fill the hat templates with pink meringue. Use a tapered spatula to smooth the meringue. Fill the dots with pink meringue to create pom-poms.

6. Remove the #8 decorating tip from the bag and replace it with a #3 decorating tip.

7. Pipe 2 columns of vertical beads on each hat, leaving about ¾ inch (2cm) of space in the middle. (See **"How to Pipe Borders"** on page 28.)

8. Remove the #3 decorating tip from the bag and replace it with a #16 decorating tip.

9. Pipe a vertical column of double shells in the middle of each hat and a column of single shells on the sides. (See **"How to Pipe Borders"** on page 28.)

10. Use a wavy motion to pipe a band on the bottom of each hat with a #16 decorating tip.

11. Fill the mitten templates with teal green meringue. Use a tapered spatula to smooth the meringue.

12. Remove the #8 decorating tip from the bag and replace it with a #3 decorating tip.

13. Pipe rows of beads on the mittens, alternating the direction of the beads with each row. Leave space at the bottom of the mittens for the band.

14. Place the baking sheets in the oven and bake the cookies for 2 hours. Remove the sheets from the oven and allow the cookies to cool completely.

15. Finely crumble a pink meringue cookie into a small dish.

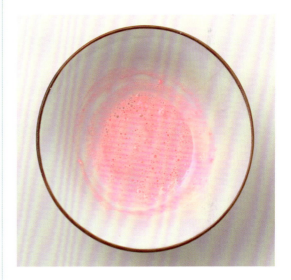

16. Stir in a few drops of water to create an edible glue.

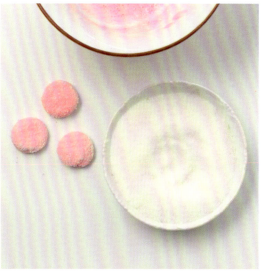

18. Apply a little bit of the edible glue on the hat cookies. Place the pom-poms on the hats and press lightly to adhere.

17. Place the sugar in a shallow dish. Use the round decorator brush to apply the edible glue to the front of the pom-poms. Dip the pom-poms in the sugar.

SNOWFLAKES

Like many of my designs, these Hanukkah cookies are inspired by my grandma's aesthetic. In the custom frame shop and art gallery she ran for more than 50 years, she carried designer gift items, including a beautiful menorah adorned with shimmering enamel, which now resides in my home. I wanted to capture the elegance of that menorah in these snowflake cookies.

WHAT YOU NEED

Chilled sheet of cookie dough (pages 44–55)
Snowflake cookie cutters
Mini 6-pointed star cookie cutter
Mini snowflake cookie cutter
1¼ cups blue flood consistency royal icing
½ cup gray medium consistency royal icing
Scribe tool
Two 12-inch (30.5cm) decorating bags and couplers
#2 decorating tip
#3 decorating tip
Edible white luster dust
Vodka, grain alcohol, or any flavor extract
Round decorator brush
Paint palette or small dish

NOTES

The icing measurements will make enough icing for 12 cookies. Adjust the amounts depending on how many cookies you need. See page 20 for the royal icing recipe.

For blue icing, add 4 to 6 drops of Royal Blue and a touch of Violet to 1¼ cups of white flood consistency icing.

To make gray icing, add a touch of Coal Black to ½ cup of white medium consistency icing.

1. Preheat the oven to 350°F (175°C).

2. Cut snowflakes from the chilled cookie dough. Cut mini 6-pointed stars and mini snowflakes from the center of the cookie dough before baking. Place the cutouts on a baking sheet.

3. Place the sheet in the oven and bake the cookies for 10 to 12 minutes. Remove the sheet from the oven and allow the cookies to cool completely before icing.

4. Fit a decorating bag with a coupler and a #3 decorating tip. Fill the bag with blue icing.

5. Flood the cookies with blue icing.

🕐 **Allow the icing to dry overnight.**

6. Fit a decorating bag with a coupler and a #2 decorating tip. Fill the bag with gray icing.

7. Pipe filigree and borders on the cookies with gray icing. (See page 197 for the filigree template.)

🕐 **Allow the icing to dry for about 1 hour.**

8. On a paint palette or in a small dish, place a small amount of white luster dust. Add a few drops of vodka and mix it with the round decorator brush.

9. Use the round decorator brush to apply the white luster dust to the entire surface of the icing.

ANYTIME COOKIES

PIZZA SLICES

The only thing better than a pizza party is a pizza party with cookies! Before serving them on edible gingham plates, give your slices a more realistic look by dusting with brown food color dust.

WHAT YOU NEED

Chilled sheet of cookie dough (pages 44–55)

3⅜ inch (8.5cm) round cookie cutter

6 baked 3⅜-inch (8.5cm) round cookies

½ cup white flood consistency royal icing

½ cup super red flood consistency royal icing

½ cup pink flood consistency royal icing

¼ cup lemon yellow flood consistency royal icing

Four 12-inch (30.5cm) decorating bags and couplers

#1 decorating tips

Edible brown matte color dust

Red edible ink marker

Scribe tool

Small knife

Ruler

Round decorator brush

NOTES

The icing measurements will make enough icing for 12 pizza slice cookies and 6 gingham plate cookies. Adjust the amounts depending on how many cookies you need. See page 20 for the royal icing recipe.

For red icing, add 4 to 5 drops of Super Red to ½ cup of white flood consistency icing.

For pink icing, add about ¼ teaspoon of the red flood consistency icing to ½ cup of white flood consistency icing. Add more red icing ¼ teaspoon at a time to make a medium shade of pink.

For yellow icing, add ½ drop of Lemon Yellow to ¼ cup of white flood consistency icing.

1. Preheat the oven to 350°F (175°C).

2. Cut 2 round cookies from the chilled sheet of cookie dough. Use a small knife to cut the rounds into 6 slices each.

3. To make the pizza crust, roll out the chilled dough into twelve ¼-inch (0.65cm) balls. Shape the balls into cylindrical shapes that are long enough to fit the curve of a slice. Brush the slices with a little bit of water and place a cylindrical shape along the curve of each slice. Gently press on them to make sure they stick. Place the slices on a baking sheet lined with parchment paper.

4. Place the sheet in the oven and bake the cookies for 8 to 10 minutes. Remove the sheet from the oven.

🕐 **Allow the cookies to cool completely.**

5. Fit 4 decorating bags with a coupler and a #1 decorating tip. Fill the bags with white, red, pink, and yellow flood consistency icing.

6. To make the gingham plates, use the red edible ink marker and a ruler to draw a ¾-inch (2cm) grid on the baked round cookies.

7. Fill every other square with pink to make a checkerboard pattern.

8. Fill the squares in every other row with white icing.

9. Fill the remaining squares with red icing.

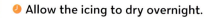 **Allow the icing to dry overnight.**

10. Pipe a wavy line of red icing along the seam of the crust.

11. Use the round decorator brush to spread the icing about halfway up the crust and a third of the way toward the point of each slice. (Clean and dry the round brush for later use in this project.)

🕐 **Allow the icing to dry for about 15 minutes.**

12. Flood the cookie with yellow icing, leaving some red icing showing.

🕐 **Allow the icing to dry for about 1 hour.**

13. Pipe small circles (whole and half) with red icing to make pepperoni. Add some tiny dots to the red icing with yellow icing.

🕐 **Allow the icing to dry for 1 hour more.**

14. Use the round decorator brush to apply brown matte color dust to the pizza cookies. Serve the pizza cookies on the gingham plates.

ICE CREAM

Enjoy a favorite summertime dessert year-round with these cookies! The trick to giving the wafer cones a realistic look is to pipe the texture underneath the flood icing. Whoever gets to eat your ice cream cookies is in for a real treat!

WHAT YOU NEED

12 baked ice cream cone–shaped cookies

3 tbsp white stiff consistency royal icing

¼ cup deep pink flood consistency royal icing

¼ cup teal green flood consistency royal icing

¼ cup purple flood consistency royal icing

1¼ cups white flood consistency royal icing

2 tbsp chocolate flood consistency royal icing (page 37)

Rainbow sprinkles

3 tipless decorating bags

Three 12-inch (30.5cm) decorating bags and couplers

#2 decorating tip

#3 decorating tip

Scribe tool

Round decorator brush

NOTES

The icing measurements will make enough icing for 12 cookies (4 of each color). Adjust the amounts depending on how many cookies you need. See page 20 for the royal icing recipe.

For pink icing, add ½ to 1 drop of Deep Pink to ¼ cup of white flood consistency icing.

For teal green icing, add 1 drop of Teal Green to ¼ cup of white flood consistency icing.

For purple icing, add 1 drop of Violet to ¼ cup of white flood consistency icing.

1. Fit a 12-inch (30.5cm) decorating bag with a coupler and a #3 decorating tip. Fill the bag with white stiff consistency icing.

2. Pipe lines on the ice cream cone cookies to create a wafer cone design.

🕐 **Allow the icing to dry for about 30 minutes.**

3. Fill the 3 tipless decorating bags with teal green, pink, and purple icing. Cut a small hole in the tip of the decorating bags.

4. Place the cookies on a wire cooling rack. Cover the cone portion of the cookies with pink, teal green, and purple icing (4 cookies in each color). Gently shake the cookies and use the round decorator brush to remove excess icing. Place the cookies on a baking sheet lined with parchment paper.

🕐 **Allow the icing to dry for about 2 hours.**

5. Fit a decorating bag with a coupler and a #2 decorating tip. Fill the bag with white flood consistency icing.

6. Fill the bottom layer of the ice cream portion of the cookies with white flood consistency icing. Pipe drips of icing over the edge of the cones.

🕐 **Allow the icing to dry for about 1 hour.**

7. Fill the top layer of the ice cream portion of the cookies with white flood consistency icing.

🕐 **Allow the icing to dry overnight.**

8. Fit a decorating bag with a coupler and a #2 decorating tip. Fill the bag with chocolate flood consistency icing.

9. Pipe a little bit of chocolate icing at the top of the ice cream on each cookie.

10. While the chocolate icing is still wet, sprinkle the rainbow sprinkles on the chocolate icing.

COFFEE & DONUTS

The best thing about these cookies is that the coffee icing actually *tastes* like coffee! Pair the coffee cookies with chocolate donut cookies for a delicious mocha-flavored treat. Don't be afraid to get creative and make your own unique latte art designs!

WHAT YOU NEED

Chilled sheet of cookie dough (pages 44–55)

3-inch (7.5cm) round cookie cutter

1-inch (2.5cm) round cookie cutter

4 baked coffee cup cookies

4 baked 3-inch (7.5cm) round cookies

¼ cup white flood consistency royal icing

¼ cup deep pink flood consistency royal icing

¼ cup teal green flood consistency royal icing

¼ cup chocolate flood consistency royal icing (page 37)

½ cup coffee flood consistency icing (page 38)

Scribe tool

Four 12-inch (30.5cm) decorating bags and couplers

#2 decorating tips

NOTES

The icing measurements will make enough icing for 12 cookies (4 of each design). Adjust the amounts depending on how many cookies you need. See page 20 for the royal icing recipe.

For pink icing, add ½ drop of Deep Pink to ¼ cup of white flood consistency icing.

For teal green icing, add ½ drop of Teal Green to ¼ cup of white flood consistency icing.

1. Preheat the oven to 350°F (175°C).

2. Cut four 3-inch (7.5cm) rounds from a chilled sheet of cookie dough. Cut 1-inch (2.5cm) holes in each round. Place the cookies on a baking sheet lined with parchment paper.

3. Place the sheet in the oven and bake the cookies for 10 to 12 minutes. Remove the sheet from the oven.

🕐 **Allow the cookies to cool completely.**

4. Fit 5 decorating bags with a coupler and a #2 decorating tip. Fill the bags with white, deep pink, teal green, coffee, and chocolate flood consistency icing.

5. To make the coffee cup cookies, flood an elongated almond shape with chocolate icing at the top of each cup, leaving room across the top for the rim.

🕐 **Allow the icing to dry for about 30 minutes.**

6. Flood the rest of the cup with teal green icing, leaving an elongated oval shape for the handle.

8. To make the latte art cookies, flood a 3-inch (7.5cm) round cookie with coffee icing, leaving about ¼ inch (0.65cm) of space around the edge.

7. Immediately pipe 4 dots in white icing down the center and stagger dots on each side.

9. Immediately pipe a latte art design outline with chocolate icing and fill the outline with white icing.

10. While the icing is still wet, drag the scribe tool through the design to blend and shape the icing.

⏱ **Allow the icing to dry for about 1 hour.**

11. Pipe an outline with teal green icing.

12. Flood a donut-shaped cookie with flood consistency icing in any color you like, creating a wavy shape as you pipe.

13. Immediately pipe lines of flood consistency icing in another color of your choice. To do this, hold the decorating bag slightly above the cookie and move it quickly back and forth as you pipe to create the look of an iced donut.

BACON & EGGS

I'm not sure anything beats bacon and eggs for breakfast, but bacon and egg cookies come pretty close! The edges of the bacon cookies are painted with edible brown color dust to give them an extra-crispy look.

WHAT YOU NEED

Chilled sheet of cookie dough (pages 44–55)
Six 2½-inch (6.25cm) baked round cookies
¾ cup white flood consistency royal icing
2 tbsp yellow flood consistency royal icing
¼ cup super red flood consistency royal icing
Three 12-inch (30.5cm) decorating bags and couplers
#2 decorating tips
#3 decorating tip
Edible brown matte color dust
Scribe tool
Small knife
Round decorator brush
Vodka, grain alcohol, or any flavor extract
Paint palette or small dish

NOTES

The icing measurements will make enough icing for 6 bacon cookies and 6 egg cookies. Adjust the amounts depending on how many cookies you need. See page 20 for the royal icing recipe.

For yellow icing, add 1 drop of Lemon Yellow and a touch of Super Red to 2 tablespoons of white flood consistency icing.

For red icing, add 2 to 3 drops of Super Red to ¼ cup of white flood consistency icing.

1. Preheat the oven to 350°F (175°C).

2. To make the bacon cookies, use a small knife to cut wavy shapes from the chilled sheet of cookie dough, about 4½ inches (11.5cm) long by 1 inch (2.5cm) wide. Place the cookies on a baking sheet lined with parchment paper.

3. Place the sheet in the oven and bake the cookies for 8 to 10 minutes. Remove the sheet from the oven.

🕐 **Allow the cookies to cool completely.**

4. Fit a decorating bag with a coupler and a #3 decorating tip. Fill the bag with white flood consistency icing.

5. Flood the baked round cookies with white icing. Set the cookies aside to begin drying.

1. Fit a decorating bag with a coupler and a #2 decorating tip. Fill the bag with red flood consistency icing. Switch the decorating tip on the white icing bag to a #2.

6. Fit a decorating bag with a coupler and a #2 decorating tip. Fill the bag with red flood consistency icing. Switch the decorating tip on the white icing bag to a #2.

7. Pipe 3 vertical wavy stripes of red icing on the bacon cookies, leaving space on both sides of the middle stripe.

8. Immediately fill the empty spaces with 2 vertical wavy stripes of white icing.

9. While the icing is still wet, use the scribe tool to marble the colors.

🕐 **Allow the bacon and eggs to dry overnight.**

10. Fit a decorating bag with a coupler and a #2 decorating tip. Fill the bag with yellow flood consistency icing.

11. Pipe a circle of yellow icing on the white cookies, about 1 inch (2.5cm) in diameter and slightly off center.

12. Place a little bit of brown matte color dust on a paint palette or in a small dish.

13. Use the round decorator brush to apply the dry dust all over the bacon surface.

14. Add a few drops of vodka, grain alcohol, or any flavor extract to the brown matte dust. Use the round decorator brush to paint the edges of the bacon cookies with the edible brown paint.

Serve your breakfast cookies with a few orange slices! The directions to make these citrus cookies are on pages 165–166.

FRUIT SLICES

These colorful fruit cookies will brighten a dreary day! Combine these slices on a single plate to create an impressive platter for dessert anytime!

WHAT YOU NEED

Chilled sheet of cookie dough (pages 44–55)

3⅜-inch (8.5cm) round cookie cutter

2½-inch (6.25cm) round cookie cutter

2-inch (5cm) round cookie cutter

½ cup light green flood consistency royal icing

2 tbsp medium green flood consistency royal icing

3 tbsp dark green flood consistency royal icing

3 tbsp white flood consistency royal icing

3 tbsp orange flood consistency royal icing

3 tbsp dark pink flood consistency royal icing

2 tbsp black flood consistency royal icing

2 tbsp brown medium consistency royal icing

Eight 12-inch (30.5cm) decorating bags and couplers

#1 decorating tips

#2 decorating tips

Scribe tool

Small knife

NOTES

The icing measurements will make enough icing for 8 watermelon cookies, 6 orange cookies, and 6 kiwi cookies. Adjust the amounts depending on how many cookies you need. See page 20 for the royal icing recipe.

For light green icing, add a touch of Leaf Green and a touch of Lemon Yellow to ½ cup of white flood consistency icing.

For medium green icing, add ½ drop of Leaf Green and a touch of Lemon Yellow food coloring to 2 tablespoons of white medium consistency icing.

For dark green icing, add 1 to 2 drops of Leaf Green and 1 drop of Lemon Yellow to 3 tablespoons of white flood consistency icing.

For orange icing, add ½ to 1 drop of Sunset Orange to 3 tablespoons of white flood consistency icing.

For dark pink icing, add a touch of Super Red to 3 tablespoons of white flood consistency icing.

For black icing, add 2 to 3 drops of Coal Black to 2 tablespoons of white flood consistency icing.

For brown icing, add 1 drop of Buckeye Brown to 2 tablespoons of white medium consistency icing.

1. Preheat the oven to 350°F (175°C).

2. Cut 2 cookies from the chilled sheet of cookie dough with the 3⅜-inch (8.5cm) round cookie cutter. Use the small knife to cut the cookies into 4 wedges for the watermelon slices.

3. Cut 3 cookies from the chilled sheet of cookie dough with the 2½-inch (6.25cm) round cookie cutter. Use the knife to cut the cookies in half for the orange slices.

4. Cut 6 cookies from the chilled sheet of cookie dough with the 2-inch (5cm) round cookie cutter. Shape the dough with your fingers to create a slightly oblong shape for the kiwis. Place all the cookies on baking sheets lined with parchment paper.

5. Place the sheets in the oven and bake the cookies for 8 to 10 minutes. Remove the sheets from the oven.

❷ **Allow the cookies to cool completely.**

6. Fit 6 decorating bags with a coupler and a #1 decorating tip. Fill the bags with light green, medium green, dark green, white, orange, and black flood consistency royal icing. Fit the remaining decorating bags with a coupler and a #2 decorating tip. Fill 1 bag with dark pink flood consistency royal icing and fill the other bag with brown medium consistency royal icing.

7. To make the orange slices, pipe a line along the curved edge of the cookie with orange icing. Pipe a line of white icing inside the orange line.

8. Immediately use the scribe tool to swirl and blend the colors together. Pipe lines with white icing to create triangle-shaped segments. Use the white icing to pipe a large dot where the segment lines meet in the middle of the cookie.

9. Fill the segments with orange icing and pipe small dots on the orange icing with white icing.

10. Immediately use the scribe tool to swirl the white dots into the orange icing.

11. To make the kiwi cookies, pipe an outline around a cookie with brown icing.

12. Fill the cookie with all 3 shades of green icing, starting with a large medium-colored green ring on the outside, a smaller dark green ring inside that, and a light green circle in the center.

13. Immediately create a starburst pattern by dragging the scribe tool through all 3 colors of icing, starting from the inside and going toward the edge. Repeat the motion again, this time moving the scribe tool from the outside and going toward the center.

14. Pipe black icing seeds on the dark green ring.

To make the kiwi seeds teeny tiny, use very light pressure on the decorating bag and barely touch the tip to the surface of the cookie to create small dots. If you're having trouble controlling the amount of icing that comes out, you can use the scribe tool to pick up a bit of black icing and then place it on the cookies.

15. To make the watermelon cookies, pipe a line of dark green icing along the curved edge of a cookie. Pipe a line of light green icing inside the dark green line.

16. Immediately use the scribe tool to swirl and blend the colors together. Pipe a line of white icing inside the blended green line.

17. Fill the rest of the cookie with dark pink icing.

18. Immediately use the scribe tool to swirl and blend the pink and white where they meet.

🕐 **Allow the icing to dry for at least 2 hours or overnight.**

19. Pipe teardrop shapes with black icing to make the watermelon seeds.

TIE-DYE T-SHIRTS

I remember attempting to tie-dye T-shirts when I was a kid. Turns out it's much easier for me to tie-dye a cookie! Just like with real tie-dye, each cookie will end up looking a little different.

WHAT YOU NEED

12 baked 3½-inch (9cm) T-shirt cookies
¼ cup white flood consistency royal icing
¼ cup super red flood consistency royal icing
¼ cup sunset orange flood consistency royal icing
¼ cup lemon yellow flood consistency royal icing
¼ cup leaf green flood consistency royal icing
¼ cup sky blue flood consistency royal icing
¼ cup purple flood consistency royal icing
7 tipless decorating bags
Scribe tool

NOTES

The icing measurements will make enough icing for 12 cookies. Adjust the amounts depending on how many cookies you need. See page 20 for the royal icing recipe.

For super red icing, add 3 to 4 drops of Super Red to ¼ cup of white flood consistency royal icing.

For sunset orange icing, add 2 to 3 drops of Sunset Orange to ¼ cup of white flood consistency icing.

For lemon yellow icing, add 2 to 3 drops of Lemon Yellow to ¼ cup of white flood consistency royal icing.

For leaf green icing, add 2 to 3 drops of Leaf Green to ¼ cup of white flood consistency royal icing.

For sky blue icing, add 2 to 3 drops of Sky Blue to ¼ cup of white flood consistency royal icing.

For purple icing, add 2 drops of Violet and 1 drop of Deep Pink to ¼ cup of white flood consistency royal icing.

1. Fill the tipless decorating bags with white, super red, sunset orange, lemon yellow, leaf green, sky blue, and purple flood consistency royal icing. Cut a small hole in the tip of each bag.

2. Starting in the center of each cookie, pipe spirals around the shirts in each color. Add fewer white spirals than the other colors.

3. Immediately outline the cookies with any color of flood consistency icing. You can use the same color for all the cookies or a different color for each cookie.

4. Starting again in the center of each cookie, drag the scribe tool through the icing, moving toward the edges.

5. Make shorter strokes in between the longer ones to give a more realistic tie-dyed effect. Use the scribe tool to pat down any peaks in the icing around the edges of the cookies.

Outline each T-shirt with a different color to create an even more vibrant assortment of cookies.

DINOSAURS

If your kids are anything like mine, they probably love dinosaurs! One of these designs has realistic textured dinosaur skin and the other has a claw reaching through the cracked shell.

WHAT YOU NEED

6 baked 3-inch (7.5cm) egg-shaped cookies
6 baked 2½-inch (6.25cm) round cookies
Dinosaur foot template (page 202)
⅓ cup gray flood consistency royal icing
⅔ cup light green flood consistency royal icing
2 tbsp dark green flood consistency royal icing
¼ cup dark green medium consistency royal icing
2 tbsp light beige stiff consistency royal icing
Five 12-inch (30.5cm) decorating bags and couplers
#1 decorating tips
#2 decorating tips
#3 decorating tips
Edible brown matte color dust
Scribe tool
Round decorator brush
Green edible ink marker

NOTES

The icing measurements will make enough icing for 12 cookies (6 of each design). Adjust the amounts depending on how many cookies you need. See page 20 for the royal icing recipe.

For gray icing, add a touch of Coal Black to ⅓ cup of white flood consistency icing.

For dark green icing, add 2 drops of Leaf Green and ½ drop of Buckeye Brown to ¼ cup plus 2 tablespoons of white medium consistency icing. Separate 2 tablespoons of dark green icing and thin it to flood consistency by following the instructions on page 19.

For light green icing, add ½ teaspoon of dark green flood consistency icing to ⅔ cup of white flood consistency icing. Add more dark green icing as needed to achieve the desired color.

For light beige icing, add a touch of Buckeye Brown to 2 tablespoons of white stiff consistency icing.

1. Fit 2 decorating bags with couplers and #3 decorating tips. Fill 1 bag with gray flood consistency royal icing. Fill the other bag with light green flood consistency royal icing. Fit another decorating bag with a coupler and a #1 decorating tip. Fill that bag with dark green flood consistency royal icing.

2. Flood an egg cookie with light green icing.

3. Immediately pipe spots in different sizes with dark green flood consistency icing.

🔸 **Allow the icing to dry for 1 hour.**

4. To make the dinosaur footprints, flood the round cookies with gray icing.

🕐 **Allow the cookies to dry overnight.**

5. Once the egg cookies have crusted over, press into the top corner of them with a finger or the back of a spoon to crack the icing.

6. Fit a decorating bag with a coupler and a #1 decorating tip. Fill the bag with dark green medium consistency icing. Fit another decorating bag with a coupler and a #1 decorating tip. Fill that bag with light beige stiff consistency royal icing.

7. Pipe a dinosaur hand coming out of one of the cracks in the icing with the dark green medium consistency icing. Pipe nails with the light beige icing.

8. Use the green edible ink marker to trace the footprint template on the gray round cookies.

9. Switch the decorating tips on the dark green and light beige icing bags to #2 decorating tips.

10. Fill the dinosaur foot with the dark green icing. Use the scribe tool to help shape the icing. Don't worry if it's not smooth.

🕐 **Allow the icing to dry for about 30 minutes.**

11. Pipe nails on the dinosaur foot with the light beige icing. Use the dark green icing to pipe lines and dots on the dinosaur foot to create texture.

🕐 **Allow the icing to dry for at least 1 hour.**

12. Use the round decorator brush to apply brown matte color dust to the footprint cookies.

MERMAID TAILS

These cookies use a brush embroidery technique and white luster dust to create shimmering mermaid tails. Serve these with Whipped White Chocolate Ganache (page 41) sandwiched between Meringue Cookies (page 53) to complete your under-the-sea platter.

WHAT YOU NEED

12 baked 4-inch (10cm) plaque cookies
Mermaid tail template (page 203)
1¼ cups purple flood consistency royal icing
⅔ cup teal green stiff consistency royal icing
¼ cup rose pink stiff consistency royal icing
Three 12-inch (30.5cm) decorating bags and couplers
#2 decorating tip
#3 decorating tips
#70 decorating tip
#101 decorating tip
Edible white luster dust
Scribe tool
Round decorator brush
Square decorator brush
Dish of water
Paper towel

NOTES

The icing measurements will make enough icing for 12 cookies. Adjust the amounts depending on how many cookies you need. See page 20 for the royal icing recipe.

For purple icing, add 2 to 3 drops of Violet to 1¼ cups of white flood consistency icing.

For teal green icing, add 1 to 2 drops of Teal Green to ⅔ cup of white stiff consistency icing.

For pink icing, add 1 drop of Rose Pink to ¼ cup of white stiff consistency icing.

1. Fit a decorating bag with a coupler and a #3 decorating tip. Fill the bag with purple flood consistency icing.

2. Flood the plaque cookies with purple icing.

🕐 **Allow the icing to dry overnight.**

3. Fit a decorating bag with a coupler and a #2 decorating tip. Fill the bag with teal green stiff consistency icing.

4. Use the scribe tool to trace the mermaid tail template on the purple icing.

5. Starting from the tip of the tail, pipe a scallop with the teal green icing.

6. Dip the square decorator brush into a dish of water and blot it on a dry paper towel. Brush the icing toward the wide end of the tail.

7. Working with 1 row at a time, repeat steps 5 and 6 for the remainder of the tail, layering the scallops as you go.

8. Fit a decorating bag with a coupler and a #3 decorating tip. Fill the bag with rose pink stiff consistency icing.

9. Pipe a bead border around the edge of the cookies with rose pink icing. (See **"How to Pipe Borders"** on page 28.)

10. Switch the decorating tip on the teal green icing to a #101 decorating tip.

11. With the wide end of the tip touching the cookie and the narrow end of the tip toward the end of the tail, use a wavy motion to pipe a ruffle along the top of the tail.

12. Switch the decorating tip on the teal green icing to a #70 decorating tip.

13. Starting at the tip of the tail and moving toward the edge of the cookie, use a wavy motion to pipe fins.

🕐 **Allow the icing to dry for at least 1 hour.**

14. Use the round decorator brush to apply white luster dust to the ruffles and fins.

BUTTERFLIES

These vibrant cookies are decorated using the wet-on-wet technique to create one smooth layer of icing. You can use any combination of colors you like for these cookies to create your own unique butterfly designs.

WHAT YOU NEED

12 baked 3-inch (7.5cm) butterfly cookies
¼ cup super red flood consistency royal icing
¼ cup sunset orange flood consistency royal icing
¼ cup lemon yellow flood consistency royal icing
¼ cup leaf green flood consistency royal icing
¼ cup sky blue flood consistency royal icing
¼ cup purple flood consistency royal icing
¼ cup black flood consistency royal icing
2 tbsp black medium consistency royal icing
8 tipless decorating bags
Scribe tool

NOTES

The icing measurements will make enough icing for 12 cookies. Adjust the amounts depending on how many cookies you need. See page 20 for the royal icing recipe.

For black icing, add 5 to 6 drops of Coal Black to ¼ cup plus 2 tablespoons of white medium consistency royal icing. Remove 2 tablespoons of black medium consistency icing and thin the rest to flood consistency by following the instructions on page 19.

For the other icings, add 4 to 5 drops of to ¼ cup of white flood consistency icing: Super Red (for red), Sunset Orange (for orange), Lemon Yellow (for yellow), Leaf Green (for green), Sky Blue (for blue), and Violet (for purple).

1. Fill 7 tipless decorating bags with a different color of flood consistency royal icing. Cut a small hole in the tip of each bag.

2. Working with 1 wing and 1 cookie at a time, outline the upper-left wing with red icing. Immediately pipe lines of orange, yellow, green, blue, and purple from the red outline toward the center of the wing.

3. Immediately outline the wing with black flood consistency icing.

6. Fill a tipless decorating bag with black medium consistency icing. Cut a small hole in the tip of the bag.

7. Pipe the body for each butterfly with black medium consistency icing.

🕐 **Allow the icing to dry for 10 to 15 minutes before piping a head for each butterfly.**

Don't clean the scribe tool between passes in step 4. This will give you a beautiful pattern of rainbow markings on the black edges of the wings.

4. While the icing is still wet, drag the scribe tool through the icing from the outside of the wing and toward the center of the butterfly.

5. Repeat steps 2 through 4 on the other wings.

🕐 **Allow the icing to dry for at least 2 hours or overnight.**

UNICORNS

You can use nearly any cookie cutter for this design. You can add some extra magic with a little gold luster dust!

1. Fit a decorating bag with a coupler and a #3 decorating tip. Fill the bag with light purple flood consistency icing.

2. Flood the plaque cookies with purple icing.

🔶 **Allow the cookies to dry overnight.**

3. Fit 3 decorating bags with a coupler and a #2 decorating tip. Fill the bags with light pink, golden brown, and white medium consistency icing.

4. Use the scribe tool to trace the unicorn template on the purple icing.

5. Fill 2 sections of the horn with golden brown icing. Fill the inside of the ears with light pink icing.

🕐 **Allow the icing to dry for about 15 minutes.**

6. Fill the remaining sections of the horn with golden brown icing. Fill the outside edges of the ears with white icing.

🕐 **Allow the icing to dry for at least 1 hour.**

7. Mix a little bit of gold luster dust with a few drops of vodka, grain alcohol, or any flavor extract on a paint palette or in a small dish.

8. Use the round decorator brush to apply the edible gold paint to the horn.

9. Fit a decorating bag with a coupler and a #352 decorating tip. Fill the bag with teal green stiff consistency icing. Fit another decorating bag with a coupler and a #16 decorating tip. Fill that bag with dark pink stiff consistency icing.

10. Pipe leaves between the ears with teal green icing.

11. Pipe 3 swirls of dark pink icing in the center of the leaves.

12. Use the black edible ink marker to draw closed eyes with eyelashes below the flowers and leaves.

13. Pipe a bead border around the edge with white icing. (See **"How to Pipe Borders"** on page 28.)

SHARKS

These ferociously delicious cookies are an example of how simple cookie cutters can create unique designs.

WHAT YOU NEED

12 baked 3-inch (7.5cm) round cookies
Shark template (page 205)
2 tbsp white flood consistency icing
1 cup dark blue flood consistency royal icing
¾ cup light blue flood consistency royal icing
¼ cup red flood consistency royal icing
2 tbsp gray flood consistency royal icing
2 tbsp pink medium consistency royal icing
1 tbsp black medium consistency royal icing
¼ cup white stiff consistency royal icing
Seven 12-inch (30.5cm) decorating bags and couplers
#1 decorating tip
#2 decorating tips
#3 decorating tips
Scribe tool
Square decorator brush

NOTES

The icing measurements will make enough icing for 12 cookies. Adjust the amounts depending on how many cookies you need. See page 20 for the royal icing recipe.

For dark blue icing, add 5 drops of Royal Blue to 1 cup of white flood consistency icing.

For light blue icing, add about 1 teaspoon of dark blue flood consistency icing to ¾ cup of white flood consistency icing. Add more dark blue icing ½ teaspoon at a time as needed.

For red icing, add 2 to 3 drops of Super Red to ¼ cup of white flood consistency icing.

For gray icing, add a touch of Coal Black to 2 tablespoons of white flood consistency icing.

For pink icing, add a touch of Super Red to 2 tablespoons of white medium consistency icing.

For black icing, add 1 to 2 drops of Coal Black to 1 tablespoon of white medium consistency royal icing.

1. Fit 2 decorating bags with a coupler and a #3 decorating tip. Fill the bags with light blue and dark blue flood consistency icing.

2. Flood just over half a round cookie with the dark blue icing, creating a wavy edge down the middle of the cookie. Immediately fill the rest of the cookie with the light blue icing.

🕐 **Allow the icing to dry overnight.**

3. Fit a decorating bag with a coupler and a #2 decorating tip. Fill the bag with white stiff consistency icing.

4. Use the scribe tool to trace the shark template on the light blue and dark blue icing.

5. To create waves, pipe a scalloped edge line along the top outer edges of the dark blue icing, leaving space for the shark in the middle.

6. Dip the square decorating brush into a dish of water and blot it on a paper towel. Brush the white icing down toward the bottom of the cookies to create texture.

7. Repeat steps 5 and 6 two more times on each side of the shark, making the waves smaller as you go toward the bottom of the cookies.

8. Fit 3 decorating bags with a coupler and a #2 decorating tip. Fill the bags with white, gray, and red flood consistency icing.

9. Fill the shark with icing: red for the mouth, white for the next section, and gray for the nose.

🕐 **Allow the icing to dry for about 1 hour.**

10. Pipe the teeth with white stiff consistency icing. Start with heavy pressure at the base of each tooth and release the pressure as you get to the tip of each tooth to create a point.

11. Fit a decorating bag with a coupler and a #2 decorating tip. Fill the bag with pink medium consistency icing. Fit another decorating bag with a coupler and a #1 decorating tip. Fill that bag with black medium consistency icing.

12. Pipe shark gums with pink icing, making sure to cover the base of the teeth. Use black icing to pipe eyes on each side of every shark's head.

TEMPLATES

BEAD
BORDERS

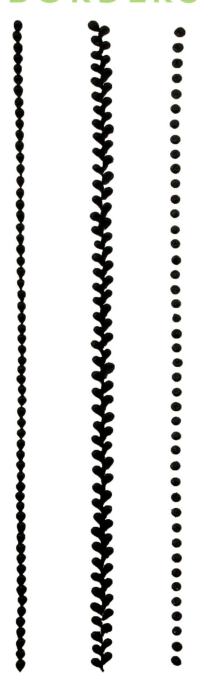

SHELL
BORDERS

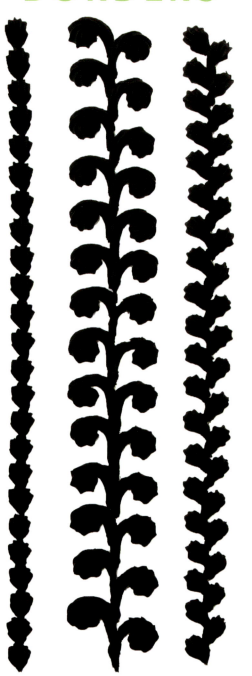

FILIGREE

COOKIE BOX

Box template side:
3.5 x 3.5 in (8.9 x 8.9cm)

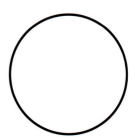

Box template lid:
1.25 in (3.2cm)
in diameter

Box template side:
5 x 3.5 in (12.7 x 8.9cm)

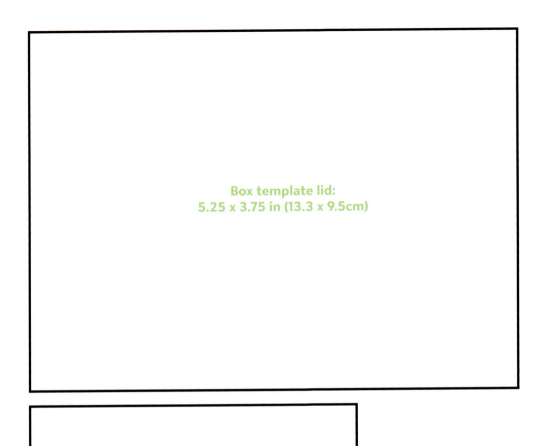

Box template lid:
5.25 x 3.75 in (13.3 x 9.5cm)

Box template bottom:
4.5 x 3.5 in (11.4 x 8.9cm)

HAPPY BIRTHDAY

2.75 in
(7cm)

3.8 in
(9.75cm)

VASE

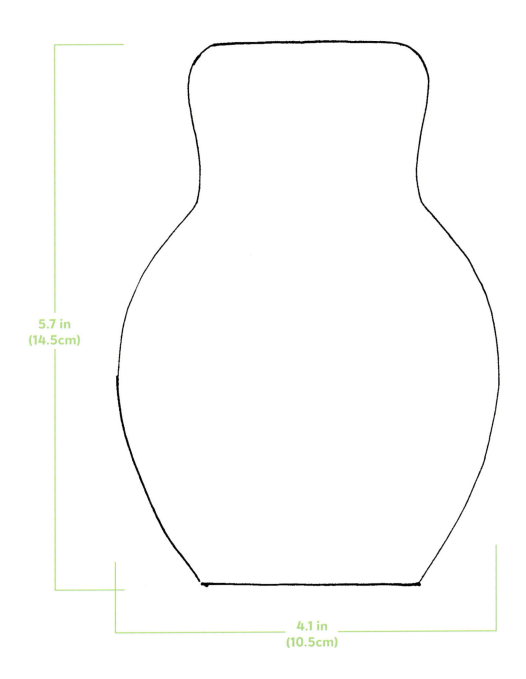

5.7 in
(14.5cm)

4.1 in
(10.5cm)

DINOSAUR FOOT

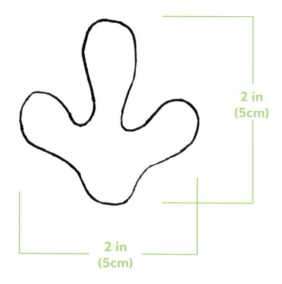

2 in
(5cm)

2 in
(5cm)

UNICORN HORN

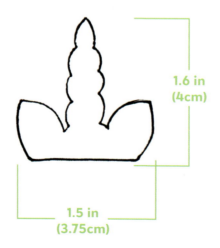

1.6 in
(4cm)

1.5 in
(3.75cm)

MERMAID TAIL

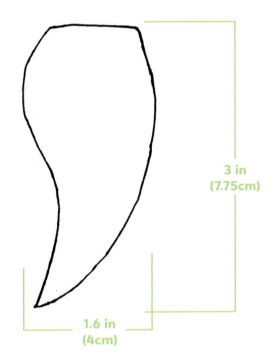

3 in
(7.75cm)

1.6 in
(4cm)

LANTERN

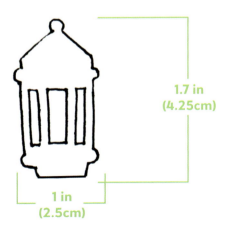

1.7 in
(4.25cm)

1 in
(2.5cm)

GRADUATION CAP & STAR

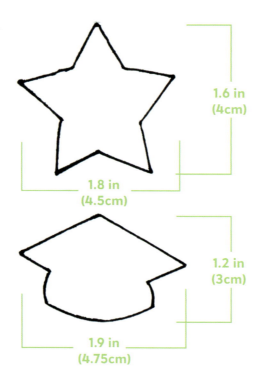

1.6 in
(4cm)

1.8 in
(4.5cm)

1.2 in
(3cm)

1.9 in
(4.75cm)

FLOWER

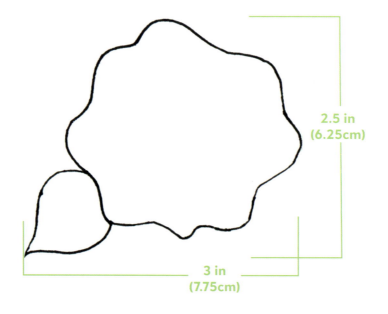

2.5 in
(6.25cm)

3 in
(7.75cm)

HAT & MITTEN

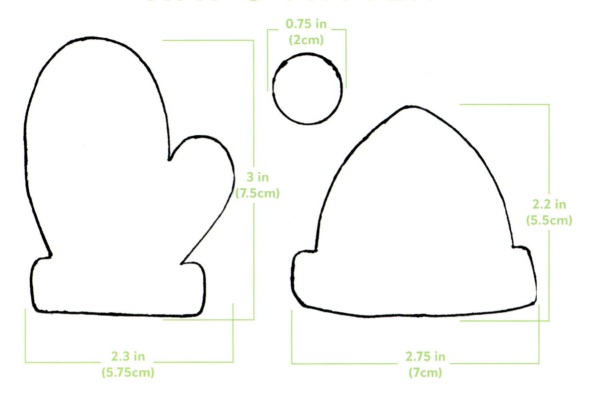

0.75 in
(2cm)

3 in
(7.5cm)

2.2 in
(5.5cm)

2.3 in
(5.75cm)

2.75 in
(7cm)

SHARK

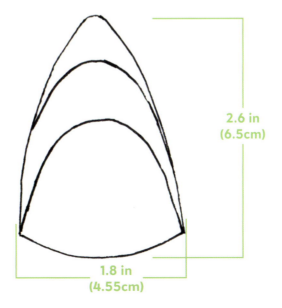

2.6 in
(6.5cm)

1.8 in
(4.55cm)

INDEX

whipped white chocolate
ganache, 41

J–K–L

jack-o'-lantern (Halloween)
cookies, 120–123

keepsake cookies, 50

lantern & star cookies (Eid),
106–109
lemon & almond cookies, 46
lime & coconut cookies, 47

M

maple cookies, 51
marbled egg cookies, 102–105
meringue cookies, 53

hats & mittens, 136–141
Mother's Day cookies, 58–61

P

parchment paper, 12–13
peanut butter cookies, 54
piping borders, 28–29
pizza slice cookies, 148–151
plaid Christmas tree
gingerbread cookies, 130–135
pumpkin cookies, 116–119

goth pumpkin cookies,
116–119
Halloween (jack-o'-lantern)
cookies, 120–123
pumpkin spice cookies, 45

R

rainbow butterfly cookies,
182–185
recipes. *See also* icing & frosting
recipes.

chocolate cookies, 48
chocolate royal icing, 37
coffee royal icing, 38
confetti cookies, 52
gingerbread cookies, 49
keepsake cookies, 50
lemon & almond cookies, 46
lime & coconut cookies, 47
maple cookies, 51
meringue cookies, 53

orange, vanilla & cardamom
cookies, 16–17
peanut butter cookies, 54
pumpkin spice cookies, 45
strawberry cookies, 55
vanilla buttercream frosting,
39, 40
vanilla cookies, 44
vanilla royal icing
with meringue (egg white
powder), 20–21
with fresh egg whites, 36
whipped white chocolate
ganache, 41
reverse shell borders, 29
rolling pins, 12
roses, piping, 32, 117
royal icing, 18–19. *See also* icing
& frosting recipes.

black, 117
colored, 22–23
painting on, 30–31, 36
vanilla, 20–21
with meringue (egg white
powder), 20–21
with fresh egg whites, 36

S

scribe tool, 12
seasonal cookies

Christmas trees, 130–135
fall bouquet, 124–129
goth pumpkins, 116–119
Hanukkah cookies
(snowflakes), 142–145
jack-o'-lantern (Halloween)
cookies, 120–123
lantern & star (Eid) cookies,
106–109
marbled eggs (Easter),
102–105
meringue hats & mittens,
136–141
snowflakes (Hanukkah
cookies), 142–145
summer BBQ (hamburger
cookies), 110–115
tulip bouquet, 98–101
Valentine's Day cookies,
94–97
sharks, 190–193

shell borders (single and
double), 29
single-bead borders, 28
snowflake (Hanukkah) cookies,
142–145
spatulas, 12
stand mixers, 12
storing and shipping, 15
strawberry cookies, 55
summer BBQ cookies, 110–115

T

templates

bead borders, 196
cookie box, 198–199
dinosaur foot, 202
filigree, 197
flower, 204
graduation cap & star, 204
happy birthday, 200
hat & mitten, 205
lantern, 203
mermaid tail, 203
shark, 205
shell borders, 196
unicorn horn, 202
vase, 201
tie-dye T-shirt cookies, 170–173
tools & equipment, 12–13
tulip bouquet, 98–101
tuxedo cookies, 62–67

U

unicorn cookies, 186–189

V

vanilla buttercream frosting, 39
vanilla cookies, 44
vanilla royal icing

with meringue (egg white
powder), 20–21
with fresh egg whites, 36

W

wedding cookies, 62–67

cakes, 63, 65–66
gowns, 63, 65–66
tuxedos, 64
whipped white chocolate
ganache, 41

ACKNOWLEDGMENTS

I dedicate this book to my daughters, Olive and Sidney.

Thank you to everyone who made this book possible!

Marc, thank you for encouraging me to do big things, for teaching me
everything I know about video production and photography,
and for always washing my royal icing– and cookie dough–coated dishes.

Mom and Dad, thank you for giving me the tools
to follow my dreams and supporting me every step of the way!

My biggest cheerleader, Grandma Jewel, you're the inspiration behind so many
of my cookie designs. Thank you for sharing all your creative ideas with me!

Emmet and Theresa, thanks for always willing to be my taste-testers!

Marlyn and Hani, our friendship has made my lonely days as a cookie decorator so much more
fun! Thank you for always being there to offer support, motivation, and a laugh.

Chris Stolle and Becky Batchelor, it's been such a pleasure
working with you on this book. Thanks for making it happen!

And thank you so much to all of you who have watched my cookie
decorating tutorials over the years and have felt inspired to create your own
works of art on a cookie canvas. I always love seeing your creations
and I appreciate your sharing your love for cookie decorating with me.